The New Americans
Recent Immigration and American Society

Edited by
Steven J. Gold and Rubén G. Rumbaut

A Series from LFB Scholarly

Immigrant Education
Variations by Generation, Age-at-Immigration, and Country of Origin

Noyna DebBurman

LFB Scholarly Publishing LLC
New York 2005

Library of Congress Cataloging-in-Publication Data

DebBurman, Noyna.
 Immigrant education : variations by generation, age-at- immigration, and country of origin / Noyna DebBurman.
    p. cm. -- (The new Americans)
 Includes bibliographical references and index.
 ISBN 1-59332-072-8 (alk. paper)
  1. Immigrants--Education--United States. 2. Children of immigrants--Education--United States. 3. Academic achievement--United States. 4. Educational surveys--United States. I. Title. II. Series: New Americans (LFB Scholarly Publishing LLC)
   LC3731.D42 2005
   371.826'912'0973--dc22

2005001038

ISBN 1-59332-072-8

Printed on acid-free 250-year-life paper.

Manufactured in the United States of America.

To my little Shruti

Table of Contents

List of Tables

List of Figures

Acknowledgements

I thank Dr. Barry Chiswick (University of Illinois at Chicago, UIC) for his invaluable support of my research, on which this book is based. I have highly valued Dr. Chiswick's continual direction in helping me think critically and work independently. I also thank Dr. Carmel Chiswick (UIC), Dr. Kevin Hollenbeck (W.E. Upjohn Institute of Employment Research), Dr. Evelyn Lehrer (UIC), Dr. Paul Pieper (UIC), and Dr. Houston Stokes (UIC) for considerable professional insight. The Upjohn Institute provided me access to the datasets used in this study. At Upjohn as well, I thank Ms. Wei-Jang Huang for programming assistance and Ms. Linda Richer for library assistance.

The final note of thanks is due to my husband, Shubhik, for his pride, enthusiasm and encouragement in all my professional endeavors.

CHAPTER 1

Introduction

Immigration is a controversial labor and social issue in the United States, with significant impact on present and future U.S. education. Recent U.S. immigration policy initiatives have produced substantial shifts in the primary immigrant-sending countries and in immigrant skills, considerably impacting the racial and ethnic composition of the U.S. population. The pattern of immigration in the last decade, coupled with the tendency of ethnic differences to persist over subsequent immigrant generations, has led to an increasing gap in educational attainment between some of the fastest growing immigrant communities in the United States. At the same time, long-term structural changes in the U.S. economy have markedly increased the importance of education, making postsecondary education a minimum requirement for any individual to compete successfully in the labor market. Thus, educational institutions in the U.S. today are faced with a twofold issue: one, to educate a larger and more diverse population and, two, to bridge the gap in educational attainment among the various ethnic groups. Immigration is poised to strongly impact the future of U.S. education, as immigrants and children-of-immigrants increasingly account for a larger proportion of school age children, highlighting the need to better understand the educational attainment of immigrants.

This book is a theoretical and empirical study of immigrant education. It deals with two aspects of immigrant education: one, the determinants of educational attainment for adult immigrants (25 to 64-years-old); two, the determinants of school enrollment for immigrant

1

children (3 to 18-years-old). The theoretical model developed to study the two distinct age groups derives from Becker's theory of human capital investment. Specifically this study uses the notion of transferability of skills to analyze educational attainment of adult immigrants, and the notion of investment in child quality and child quantity to analyze school enrollment of immigrant children.

A growing body of literature on economic assimilation of immigrants has focused on human capital transfer, human capital investment, and labor market adjustment of immigrants. A significant portion of this literature (Chiswick, 1977; 1978a; Hashmi, 1987; Borjas, 1982) examines the foreign-born relative to the native-born, and importantly, has focused on the length of time it takes for the foreign-born to assimilate into the host country both economically and socially. Additionally, the intergenerational aspects of assimilation have also been explored to some detail. Chiswick (1988) studied the intergenerational effect of ethnic background on educational outcomes, and Borjas (1992) examined the intergenerational transfer of human capital and earnings among ethnic groups.

Research on immigrant educational attainment is a fairly recent phenomenon. A persistent limitation is that most studies fail to distinguish between the different generations of U.S. residence. Second-generation immigrants (*i.e.* those born in the U.S. of immigrant parents) are typically grouped together with first-generation immigrants (*i.e.* those who are immigrants themselves) or with native-parentage adults and children (*i.e.* those who are U.S. born with U.S.-born parents). Several reasons exist as to why an analysis by immigrant generation is crucial in understanding immigrant educational attainment. First, a continuous influx of immigrants into the U.S. in the past three decades has resulted in a significant proportion of the U.S. population today being comprised of second-generation immigrants (*i.e.* children-of-immigrants). Second, while first-generation immigrants receive little or none of their education in the United States, second-generation immigrants and native-parentage adults receive all their education in the United States. Third, the second-generation immigrants are a distinct group: they are born in the United States, but unlike native-parentage adults, ethnic group influences play a crucial role in the formation of their human capital. An examination of educational attainment by immigrant generation will enable us to understand if attainment increases with each successive generation, and will help recognize the intergenerational impact of ethnic background on educational outcomes, providing possible avenues to reduce the existing gap in educational attainment gap between different ethnic groups.

This study makes a significant contribution to the immigration literature by conducting a systematic analysis of schooling acquisition of immigrants by immigrant generation. In addition, this book also examines the effects of country-of-origin and age-at-immigration on immigrant education. For adult immigrants, schooling acquisition refers to total years of schooling, and for immigrant children schooling acquisition refers to school enrollment. While economists have explored some aspects of adult educational attainment, the school enrollment of immigrant children remains a vastly unexplored arena.

For adult immigrants, education typically has two components – schooling completed in the home country prior to immigration, and schooling acquired in the destination country after immigration. Three studies on post-immigration schooling investment of immigrants stand out: Borjas (1982) and Hashmi (1987) have examined the determinants of post-immigration investment in education in the United States, and Chiswick and Miller (1994) have conducted a similar study for Australia. Both the U.S.-based studies have focused on men alone. But while Hashmi examined foreign-born men between 18 and 64 years who migrated at age 15 and above, Borjas focused on Hispanic male immigrants between 18 and 64 years. Moreover, the data used in both these studies necessitated that years of schooling in the United States be measured as a residual. Chiswick and Miller's analysis is more comprehensive since they analyzed the determinants of post-migration investment for all adult immigrants between 25 and 64 years in Australia and used data that provided explicit information on pre- and post-migration schooling. The goal of this study is to focus on total schooling acquired (a stock concept) by adult immigrants rather than on post-migration investment in schooling (a flow concept).

For immigrant children, this study examines enrollment of two age groups: one, preschoolers (3 to 5 age group) and two, high school teenagers (16 to 18 age group). Since enrollment in school is compulsory in most states for children between 6 and 15 years, enrollment rates in this age range are close to 100 percent; consequently this age group is not the focus of our research. Youth education research in economics has typically concentrated on issues such as investment in child quantity versus child quality, school performance, and teenage dropout rates. These studies have examined differences by race, but rarely make comparisons between different immigrant ethnic groups, or immigrant generational effects.[1] In particular, research on preschool enrollment among different immigrant groups is lacking. The present study aims to fill this void in the literature by representing one of the first attempts to develop an empirical model to study preschool enrollment and high school enrollment among immigrants, by country-of-origin, and by immigrant generation.

CHAPTER 2

Review of Schooling Acquisition Literature

To formulate a theoretical model for this study, a diverse body of work that has relevance to schooling acquisition was explored. This chapter first reviews studies directly pertaining to immigrant school attainment and school enrollment; followed by research on immigrant language acquisition; lastly, diverse topics which affect schooling attainment, including investment in child quality versus quantity and female labor-force participation, are discussed. These topics will be discussed as part of the following three logical categories:

1) Investment in Schooling
2) Investment in Language
3) Investment in Child Quality and Child Quantity

INVESTMENT IN SCHOOLING

In discussing the existing literature on investment in schooling, it is easiest to classify this body of work into two broad groups, based on the investigator's research methodology and/or discipline. Anthropologists and sociologists have led the major work in this field and form the first group, while, in more recent years, economists have also become engaged to form the second group.

Socio-Anthropological Analysis of Investment in Schooling

Among sociologists and anthropologists, two theories have dominated research on educational attainment of U.S. immigrants: the cultural discontinuity theory and the cultural ecology theory. Proponents of the cultural discontinuity theory believe that immigrant youth are disadvantaged due to language, cultural, and social interactional conflicts between home and school (Carter and Segura, 1979; Trueba, 1987; Perlmann, 1988). In their studies, they find that immigrant educational attainment increases with increased duration of stay in the United States and more acculturation to American society. On the other hand, cultural-ecological theorists believe that immigrant educational attainment is affected by a complex interaction of multiple factors that include motivation to immigrate, perceptions of opportunity, and labor market payoff for attainment (Ogbu, 1978; 1987; Ogbu and Matute-Bianchi, 1986). These latter theorists propose that ethnicity and generation together determine educational attainment. However, more recently, some studies have produced findings that do not always fully agree with one or the other of these two theories, yet they represent important advances and are described below.

Several key studies specify that immigrant generation plays an important role in educational attainment and school performance (Portes and Rumbaut, 1990; Rong and Grant, 1992; Kao and Tienda, 1995). Usually, second-generation youth perform better academically than first-generation youth or native youth. But, first-generation youth who immigrate at very young ages often exhibit educational attainment similar to those attained by the second-generation youth. Most such studies also point out substantial effects of ethnicity on educational attainment (Rong and Grant, 1992; Kao, Tienda, and Schneider, 1996). Asians outperform other groups in attainment (Hirschman and Wong, 1986; Lee and Rong, 1988). Hispanic students, in particular, have lower achievement levels and higher dropout rates compared to Asians and non-Hispanic whites (Arias, 1986; Velez, 1989). Furthermore, Rong and Grant (1992) examined the combined effects of immigrant generation and ethnicity on educational attainment. Their study found that immigrant generation affects youth educational attainment, but this influence is inconsistent across generation and ethnicity.

In a study of factors affecting high school completion of immigrants and native-born ethnic groups, White and Kaufman (1997) found that "social capital" is the crucial factor in high school completion. They created a socio-economic status variable based on parent's education, parent's occupation, and family income. They also tested five social capital variables (parents are present, parents monitor, talk to parents, number of siblings, siblings in college). The authors indicated that test scores and grades affect the probability of dropping out, but social capital, as measured by parent's characteristics and behavior, continues to be significant even after controlling for these factors. In fact, social capital characteristics can outweigh the effects of generation, ethnicity, duration of stay in the United States and English language usage. Importantly, the negative effects on dropout rates associated with foreign birth and lower socio-economic status may also be offset by social capital.

Lastly, Rumbaut (1995) specifically explored the educational performance of children of immigrants. This analysis, based on the Children of Immigrants Longitudinal Study (CILS), was a multifaceted investigation of the educational performance and social, cultural, and psychological adaptation of children of immigrants in the United States. CILS, directed by A. Portes and R.G. Rumbaut, studied teenage youths in two key areas of immigrant settlement in the United States: Southern California and South Florida. The original 1992 survey was administered to 8th and 9th grade students; the 1995-96 survey followed the same students in high school. Rumbaut found that immigrant children not only made rapid positive adjustments; they outperformed native-born high school students in grades as well as graduation rates. These findings support earlier evidence (Ogbu, 1974; 1987; 1991) that suggest that some minority groups perform very well in school in spite of facing obstacles because of built-in language and cultural differences within the school system.

Economic Analysis of Investment in Schooling

Although their foray into immigration research has been more recent, economists have made significant contributions focusing on two aspects of educational attainment: one, post-migration schooling of immigrants (Schultz, 1984; Hashmi, 1987; Khan, 1997; Chiswick and Miller, 1994; Chiswick and Sullivan, 1995); and the two patterns of the education attained by immigrants in their country-of-origin (Funkhouser and Trejo, 1995; Cohen, Zach, and Chiswick, 1997). The key findings that have emerged from the post-migration literature are that age-at-immigration coupled with duration of residence in the host country is a primary determinant of investment in schooling. Chiswick (1978a) indicates that immigrants tend to make their human capital investments within the first few years of arriving in the host country. Moreover, as the duration of residence in the U.S. increases, the years of post-migration schooling increase, but at a decreasing rate (Chiswick and Miller, 1994; Khan, 1997). Enrollment rates of immigrants are higher in the first few years following immigration and decline thereafter (Chiswick and Miller, 1994; Cobb-Clark, et al., 2004). Most studies of post-migration investment agree that foreign-born individuals from non-English speaking countries invest more in post-migration schooling than foreign-born people from English-speaking countries (Chiswick and Miller, 1994; Khan, 1997; Cobb-Clark et al., 2004). Furthermore, human capital investments tend to be lower when the cost of to-and-from migration to the home country is low (Borjas, 1982; Chiswick and Miller, 1994; Duleep & Regets, 1999).

Recently, several new studies have considerably heightened our understanding of post-migration schooling. Schaafsma and Sweetman (2001) investigated the impact of age-at-immigration on educational attainment. They found that return to education varies systematically across age-at-immigration: immigrants arriving when they are between ages 15 and 18 acquire less total education than those who immigrate at a younger or older age. According to the authors, "adjusting to a new environment near the transition out of high school may have a permanent effect." Furthermore, Gang and Zimmerman (2000) indicated that the gap in educational attainment between immigrants and their comparable German cohort is much smaller in the second-generation compared to the gap in the first-generation, implying that assimilation exists in the acquisition of education. This finding is in line with Schultz (1984) and Betts and Lofstrom (2000), who found that the schooling level of children-of-immigrants converges toward that of the children-of-natives. According to Schultz (1984), while immigrant children go through an initial period of difficulty, within a decade they surpass the children of native parents. Sanford and Seeborg (2003) find that both age-at-arrival and the ethnic capital, through their influence on educational attainment and language proficiency, affects immigrants' standard of living. Immigrants who arrive as children receive greater returns to human capital investments than immigrants who arrive as young adults. Also, immigrants who arrive as children are affected less than young adult immigrants by the ethnic capital of their group in the United States. Riphahn (2003) focuses on the German-born children of immigrants. She finds that their educational attainment, measured by current enrollment or highest completed degree is significantly below that of natives. Moreover, the gap in educational attainment between the two groups increases over time except when the immigrant's country-of-origin is controlled for. Ramakrishnan's (2004) study is unique in that he narrows down the definition of the traditional second-generation immigrant. Most studies define second-generation immigrants as native-born residents who have at least one foreign-born parent. He defines second-generation immigrants as native-born residents with both parents foreign-born or non-U.S. born. Those native-born residents who have at least one U.S.-born parent are called the 2.5 generation. In comparing the 2.0 and 2.5 generation with the native born with two native born parents, Ramakrishnan finds that the 2.5 generation has nearly one additional year of schooling compared to the 2.0 generation. Also, the rate of high school dropouts among native-borns with two immigrant parents is twice as high compared to native-borns with an immigrant mother and a native-born father. The presence of a native-born parent, especially of a native-born mother, makes a significant difference in the likelihood that the children of immigrants graduate from high school and obtain college degrees.

The studies on patterns of educational attainment indicated that the schooling level of immigrants to the United States exceeds the national average (Chiswick, 1978b; Portes and Rumbaut, 1990). In studying immigrant cohorts, Borjas (1987) described a decline in the schooling level of immigrants in the 1970s, but Cohen, Zach, and Chiswick (1997) found that during the 1980s, this trend had stopped and been reversed.

INVESTMENT IN LANGUAGE

In recent years, the role of language has increasingly gained importance in studies of labor market assimilation of immigrants. Language capital – a specific component of human capital – is the ability of an immigrant to communicate in the language of the host country. Consideration of the literature involving investment in language is important to the research on schooling investment for two reasons: first, some of the factors that affect language acquisition may also affect schooling acquisition for adult immigrants; secondly, proficiency in the dominant language of the host country may have direct effects on school enrollment and academic performance for immigrant children.

The first studies in language primarily examined the significance of English fluency on the earnings of immigrants. Grenier (1984) and Tainer (1988) found that English language proficiency has a significant positive influence on earnings for all ethnic groups. Similarly, Funkhouser (1995) found that U.S. immigrants who were fluent in English earned 20 to 30 percent more than those who were non-fluent. Furthermore, Park (1999) found that immigrants fluent in English received higher returns from education and experience acquired prior to immigration.

Kossoudji (1988) and Chiswick and Miller (1992) have offered a broader perspective on this issue. Kossoudji claimed that English language deficiency imposes a real cost on immigrant workers by reducing earnings as well as altering occupational opportunities. Chiswick emphasized that proficiency in destination specific skills, including the destination language, is vital in the successful economic assimilation of immigrants. Yet immigrants differ widely in how much destination specific skills they acquire. This variability prompts the question – why do some immigrants never acquire the dominant language? In an effort to answer this question, in several recent studies, Chiswick and Miller (1992, 1995, 1998, 1999, 2001) examined the factors that influence an immigrant's decision to invest in "language capital" by studying the process of language acquisition for the United States, Canada, Australia, and Israel. They found that the determinants of language proficiency are similar for these countries; similarities persist even when the analysis was performed using different data sets for the same country and using similar specifications for different countries. These studies have provided valuable insight into the differential extent to which immigrants invest in language and other destination-specific skills.

Several key findings have emerged from Chiswick and Miller's studies. First, dominant-language fluency was found to vary with economic incentives, efficiency, and exposure (Chiswick and Miller, 1992; 1995; 1998; 1999). Dominant language fluency was directly related to an immigrant's level of schooling and duration in the destination, and was inversely related to an immigrant's age at immigration. Dustmann (1994, 1997) also established this positive effect of schooling on language for Germany. But, while Chiswick and Miller (1994) indicated that pre-and post-migration education have the same effect on language fluency, Dustmann (1997) found that education acquired by immigrants in Germany has a stronger effect on language abilities than does education received in their country-of-origin. Chiswick and Miller (1992) also emphasized that as the duration of stay increases, the advantageous position of those with more schooling diminishes. Besides, duration of stay has the largest partial effect on those who immigrate at an older age, and on those with less schooling.

Secondly, using Australian data, Chiswick and Miller (1994) found that education has a stronger effect on reading and writing skills than it does on speaking skills. In further support of this notion, Dustmann (1997) determined that formal education has a greater influence on writing abilities than on speaking abilities for immigrants to Germany. Moreover, Chiswick and Miller (1994) found that better educated immigrants are less likely to live in ethnic enclaves. In a later study, Chiswick and Miller (1995, 1998) discovered that fluency rates tend to be higher if the cost of migration to the destination country and emigration from the destination country is high. Based on a study of male immigrants in Canada, Chiswick and Miller (2003) find that there is complementarity between language skills and both schooling and pre-immigration experience. In other words, greater proficiency in the official language enhances the effects on earnings of schooling and pre-immigration labor market experience.

Thirdly, two additional factors were found to determine dominant language proficiency: language spoken at home and language spoken in the area where the immigrant lives (Chiswick and Miller, 1992; 1998). In supporting the importance of language spoken at home, marriage was found to have a positive impact on the English language fluency of men and a negative or zero effect for women. However, the strength of these impacts varied depending on when the immigrant was married (pre- or post-migration) and whether the spouse had the same mother tongue. Furthermore, the presence of children positively affected the English language skills of adult men (Chiswick and Miller, 1999) but either had no effect (Chiswick and Miller, 1999) or lowered women's level of English language proficiency (Chiswick and Miller,

1998). The negative effect became larger as the number of children in the household increased and the age of the children increased. In supporting the importance of language spoken in the area in which the immigrant lives, Chiswick and Miller (1992) determined that fluency rates tend to be lower for immigrants who live in ethnic enclaves where their native language is spoken with greater frequency. However, the adverse effects of a language enclave are strongest during the initial years of immigration, for those immigrating at an older age and for those with lower levels of education. Other studies have also emphasized the negative effects associated with living in ethnic enclaves. In particular, Dustmann (1994) attributes the lower fluency of Turkish immigrants in Germany to their being the largest non-German immigrant group and their reduced exposure to German due to residence in ethnic enclaves. Evans (1986) suggests that immigrants with large enclaves have less economic incentive to acquire dominant language fluency.

Finally, as emphasized by Chiswick and Miller (1998, 2001), 'linguistic distance' plays an important role in language acquisition. This correlation derives from the evidence in the linguistics literature that the actual "distance" between the native and the target languages acts as a constraint on learning a language. According to Corder (see Ellis, 1994) "other things being equal, the mother tongue acts differentially as a facilitating agency. Where the mother tongue is formally similar to the target language, the learner will pass rapidly along the developmental continuum, than where it differs." Chiswick and Miller (1998) interpret this concept of linguistic distance in economic terms by stating that the greater the linguistic difference between the destination and the origin language (or immigrant's mother tongue), the lower will be the efficiency in language acquisition.

Past and recent research on language acquisition has predominantly focused on the language skills of adult immigrants, with few studies on children. A notable exception is Sweetman (1998), who makes an important contribution to the literature on language capital by relating immigrant children's language ability to their test outcomes in the Third International Math and Science Survey. He found that individual language skill (self-reported language use at home) as well as average language skill in the student's school had large and independent effects in test outcomes. A second important variable was the neighborhood effect – schools with higher percentages of immigrants, and/or those who did not speak the dominant language (language of instruction) at home were associated with reduced outcomes. However, if the non-English-speaking fraction was controlled for, the immigrant percentage could have a positive impact on a student's test outcomes, implying that immigrants with good English skills can exert a positive influence on outcomes. In added support, schools with a high percentage of students whose fathers possess university degrees achieved higher outcomes. Furthermore, Dustmann (1997) notes that father's education has a strong and positive influence on the acquisition of language capital. This finding is consistent with studies on intergenerational mobility (Zimmerman, 1992; Borjas, 1992), which suggests that the educational background of parents is relevant for the offspring's educational achievement as well as for his/her acquisition of other types of human capital.

In summary, research in language proficiency indicates that an immigrant's individual characteristics (exposure to the dominant language prior to immigration, age at immigration, education level) as well as group effects (size of immigrant community, linguistic distance) affect the costs of, and benefits to, language acquisition. This relative cost associated with the process of acquisition in turn determines the extent to which immigrants invest in 'language capital.'

INVESTMENT IN CHILD QUALITY AND CHILD QUANTITY

Child attainment is typically measured by school performance and high school completion during teenage years, and by post-secondary education, occupation, or income levels during young adulthood. Research on child attainment is relevant to the study of immigrant schooling acquisition for two reasons. Educational attainment in youth is shaped largely by circumstances, including the allocation of parental resources experienced during early childhood. Therefore, to understand the factors that impact educational attainment, it is important to study preschool human capital acquisition (Tach and Farkas, 2003). Moreover, variations in parental resources among diverse ethnic and immigrant groups may help explain the systematic differences in school enrollment patterns by immigrants. A significant body of literature that studies factors determining child attainment has accumulated in the past two decades but for the purpose of this study, only those papers that relate to educational outcomes and preschool enrollment will be reviewed.

In examining the process of child attainment, economists have mostly relied on the Becker-type model of family behavior. Becker and Lewis (1973) and Becker and Tomes (1976) view the family as an economic unit that employs real inputs (time and money) to maximize utility for its members. Arguably, Becker's (1964) most important contribution is the concept that parents obtain utility from the quality as well as the quantity of their children. The term 'quality' is typically used as a measure of children's characteristics such as educational attainment. Household utility is thus formulated as a function of the number of children, quality of children, and composite goods.

In exploring the interaction of the quantity and quality of children, Becker and Lewis (1973) and Becker (1967) emphasized that an increase in quality is more expensive if there are more children (since the increase has to apply to more units); similarly an increase in quantity is more expensive if the children are of higher quality, since higher-quality children cost more. Becker and Tomes (1976) further indicate that an individual's income goes more towards increasing the quality of their children, rather than increasing the quantity of children. However, an increase in income leads to an increase in quality (rather than quantity of children) only if the quality income elasticity is relatively high and the quantity income elasticity is relatively low.

Fan (1997) expands on the Becker-Lewis model of the tradeoff between the quantity and quality of children to explain why the quality income elasticity is likely to be relatively high and the quantity income elasticity relatively low. Fan builds on the existing assumption that 'production' of the quantity of children is time-intensive (Becker, 1967) and that the quality of children is money-intensive (Becker and Tomes, 1976). Fan persuasively argues that when people have low incomes they are relatively "time abundant" but face substantial financial constraints; and as people's income increases they become more "money abundant" but more and more "time scarce." This argument states that when incomes are low, the income elasticities of quantity (of children and of material goods) are larger than income elasticities of qualities. On the other hand, when people's incomes reach a certain level, the quality income elasticity becomes high and the quantity income elasticity is very low, zero, or negative.

Leibowitz (1974) builds on the general Becker framework to present an economic model of the process of children's attainments, which provides additional insight for empirical work. According to this model (Figure 1), children inherit some of the genetic characteristics of the parents. Importantly, parent's education, together with their genetic characteristics, determines the quality and quantity of time inputs to the child. Furthermore, parental ability and education also determines family income, which, in turn, influences the quantity and quality of time as well as commodity inputs. These time and money inputs together comprise "home investment." Home investment together with child ability ultimately determines school attainment. Finally, schooling influences post-schooling investment, which, in turn affects children's earnings and income.

Figure 1: Causal Model Depicting Parental Investment in Children. Adapted From Leibowitz (1974)

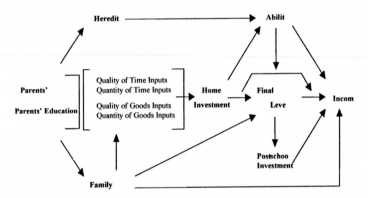

Both economic and other social science perspectives have emphasized the role of the family (particularly, family background and family composition) in child educational attainment. With respect to family background, three factors emerge as important. First, several studies (Hill and Duncan, 1987; Haveman et al., 1991; Manski et al. 1992) indicate that parental human capital, typically measured by their years of schooling completed, is a primary determinant of a child's educational attainment. Leibowitz (1972) supports this dominant effect of parental education by finding that quantity of time inputs is positively related to parental education. Schoggen and Schoggen

(1968) reinforce this by finding that the quality of time inputs is also positively related to parent education. Additionally, Manski et al. (1992) find that mother's education has a stronger impact on the child's attainment than does father's education. Second, many studies (Hill and Duncan, 1987; Duncan, 1994; Behrman et al., 1995) observe that family income is positively associated with the educational attainment of the child. Lastly, the effect of the mother's work on child attainment has yielded mixed findings.[2] While some studies find a negative effect (Krein and Beller, 1988), others find no effect (Leibowitz, 1977; Stafford, 1987) or a positive effect (Haveman et al., 1991).

Two issues appear vital with regard to family composition. First, birth order and child spacing influence child attainment in families. Hanushek (1992) argues that depending on child spacing, the same completed family size corresponds to differing parental time inputs to children during preschool and schooling periods. Second, family structure is believed to be significant to child attainment; however, contrasting views prevail. Glick and White (2003a, 2003b), Krein and Beller (1988) and Haveman et al. (1991) point out that living in a one-parent family is negatively related to the level of schooling attained. In contrast to the negative effect of single-parent families, Stafford (1987) and Hanushek (1992) find that the absence of a father does not affect educational performance of children. Jepsen & Jepsen (2001) find that adult occupation, religion, and family structure (two-parent family and only child status) generally have significant positive effects on educational attainment. Cardak and McDonald (2004) found that father's occupation and both parents' education levels are important determinants of the educational attainment of their children, as is the number of siblings present in the household.

Chiswick (1988), Borjas (1992), and Dicks and Sweetman (1999) have contributed significantly to extending the literature by studying the quality-quantity tradeoff and the intergenerational aspect of human capital investment at the level of ethnic groups. Chiswick (1988) finds that for the more successful groups, the mother's labor force participation rate is lower, particularly when the child is young. This relationship is consistent with Chiswick's earlier finding (1986) that the higher levels of schooling of American Jews is related to Jewish parents making greater investment in their children's home-produced capital. Jewish women (compared to other women) made greater investments of their own time in the home-produced human capital of their children when the children were young (and time-intensive) and they worked more (than other women) when their children were older (and goods-intensive). Higher female labor force participation rates increased child quality through increased family money income but it came at the cost of parental time. When a child is young, time is considered more important than money income in raising child quality.

Dicks and Sweetman (1999) found that for both men and women, fertility of one generation is inversely related to educational outcomes of the subsequent generation, both in terms of level of schooling and return to schooling. Besides, higher levels of education and income for an ethnic group in one generation are associated with higher levels of education and higher returns to education for that ethnic group in the next generation. These findings are consistent with the hypothesis that differences in attainment arise from differential home investments (family inputs) in children; and the level of investment per child tends to be higher in smaller families. They are also consistent with earlier studies: Borjas (1992) indicated that the skills of one generation are shaped not only by their parents' skills, but also by the average skill level of the ethnic group in the parents' generation (referred to as ethnic capital). Borjas, Dicks, and Sweetman argue that such intergenerational correlation leads to a slow convergence in income levels across ethnic groups. Interestingly, these views are consistent with an early observation by Chiswick (1988) that a positive relationship exists between educational attainments across generations, implying intergenerational transfer of human wealth (income, schooling and occupational status).

The studies on child quality discussed so far focused on two issues, namely outcomes (determinants of children's performance in school, and their attainment as adults), and inputs (time and money resources devoted to children). Earlier research on 'input' usually focused on the effects of variation in maternal time input on children of different ages. However, the dramatic increase in female labor force participation, especially employment of mothers with young children, has made non-maternal care for young children a topic of increasing interest.

The child care literature typically distinguishes between two major child care arrangements. One is a formal day care center arrangement (referred to as center-based care), usually run by trained individuals, and offering a variety of educational and developmental programs. The second is an informal child-care arrangement involving unpaid/paid care by a relative or paid care in one's own home or a babysitter's home (referred to as family day care). Though each mode of child care has its pros and cons, the psychology literature points to the advantage of preschoolers attending center-based day care over alternative arrangements (Berk, 1985; Howes, 1983; Ruopp et al., 1979). Day care centers allow children the opportunity to interact with peers, and typically expose children to several formal learning experiences that are beneficial for early childhood development. However, compared to informal arrangements, day care centers are a more expensive, and yet less flexible (fixed time, no discounts for additional siblings) arrangements, making it a less attractive option for some parents.

The two most commonly researched areas in child care are the price and quality of available substitutes for maternal time. The seminal work in child care done by Heckman (1974), which examined the link between child care costs and female labor force participation, found a negative effect of cost of child care on labor supply. Robins and Spiegelman (1978) found demand for paid child-care to be responsive to price and income. Blau and Robins (1988) provided the first direct evidence that child-care use is responsive to its price, and also indicated that the labor force participation of married mothers as well as other family members is responsive to child care price. They found that higher child care costs are negatively related to the probability that mothers will participate in the labor force. Duncan and Hill (1977) and Lehrer (1983, 1989) established a strong effect of mother's earnings on the use of center-based care, and they attributed this relation to high value of maternal time, and the reliability of formal day care.

Powell (2002) contributes to the child care literature by distinguishing how part-time and full-time work is affected differently by child care costs. The marginal cost of paid care and the availability of unpaid care decreases with hours, thus implying that demand for paid care is a function of hours worked. Powell finds that child care costs have a stronger negative impact on the probability that a mother works full-time. Powell (2002) examines the impact of wage rates, child care prices, and other demographic variables on the joint employment-childcare decisions of married mothers. As expected, child care prices for center, sitter, and relative care were found to have significant negative effects on the probability of working, and on the likelihood of using each respective mode of care. Furthermore, Connelly and Kimmel (2003) indicate that the probability of using center-based care increases with full-time employment of mothers, and mothers employed part-time show a greater reliance on relative care. Consequently, for both married and single women, part-time employment is less sensitive to price of child care than full-time employment. This differential effect of price of child care on full-time versus part-time employment is in agreement with earlier studies, which established that informal child care arrangements are more common among mothers working part-time (Lehrer, 1983, 1989), while mothers working full-time are more likely to choose center-based/nursery school (Lehrer, 1989; Leibowitz et al. 1988; Ribar, 1992). Moreover, as Brayfield and Hofferth (1995) indicate, both cultural and economic factors influence the purchase of child care by employed mothers. According to the authors, black mothers were less likely than white or Hispanic mothers to purchase care, holding economic resources and family structure constant. Leibowitz et al. (1988) also found that women with Hispanic or other foreign backgrounds are more likely to have relatives care for their children. Han and Waldfogel (2001) find that child care costs have strong effects on employment of women with preschool-aged children and these effects are larger for single mothers than for married mothers.

Leibowitz et al. (1988) was the first to point out that child care arrangements should be analyzed by age since infants (0-2 years), preschoolers (3-5 years), and older children have different care and development needs, thereby implying that the optimal form of care is likely to differ by age. Several studies emphasize low ratio of children to adults as a requisite of quality care for infants/toddlers (Francis and Self, 1982; Philips and Howes, 1989). Since paid care in the child's home represents one-to-one care, it is viewed as the most appropriate mode of care for infants. Preschoolers, on the other hand, are believed to benefit from interaction with other children and adults trained in early childhood education (Berk, 1985).

Lehrer (1989) specifically examined the determinants of child care mode choice for preschool age children and found that the probability of center care increases with an increase in mother's wage and markedly with an increase in mother's schooling. An increase in father's income level also raises the probability of using center-based care. Another important factor is the number of siblings – presence of more than two siblings decreases the probability of choosing center care for a preschooler.[3] However, when the preschooler has one sibling, the age of the sibling also matters. Since parents tend to make the same arrangements for all children, the presence of a sibling aged 3 to 5 increases the probability that a preschooler is enrolled in center care compared to the presence of either a younger or older sibling.

Lehrer's findings are in line with the Leibowitz et al. (1988) finding that income and education are strong determinants of labor force participation and child care choice. According to Lehrer, the more educated mothers are more likely to view center care as an optimal arrangement for their preschoolers. Leibowitz et al. (1988) also established that women who have higher education are more likely to work, but they are also more likely to provide the most age-appropriate care for their children. However, the education effect is more ambiguous for less educated, low earning mothers since they do not have the buying power to afford the age-appropriate care.

In summary, much of the research on child attainment and child care emphasizes that decisions made by parents regarding the generation of economic resources (e.g., labor supply and income) and the allocation of these resources (consumption, asset accumulation, investment in children) directly affects the attainments of children in the family. Child quality investment models, when applied to ethnic groups, suggest that fertility rates, female labor force participation and socioeconomic conditions (parental education and income) in one generation are important variables for analyzing group outcomes in the next generation (Chiswick, 1998).

The human capital acquired in formal preschool settings may be cognitive skills or noncognitive behavioral patterns, or a combination of the two.[4] From the point of view of the individual, either skill is productive if it enhances future educational attainment and eventual labor market success.

CHAPTER 3

Theoretical Framework

The empirical framework for analyzing the schooling acquisition of U.S. immigrants is developed based on the theory of the investment in human capital and the theory of the demand for schooling.

THEORY OF HUMAN CAPITAL INVESTMENT

This study draws on the theory of investment in human capital developed by Schultz (1961) and Becker (1964). Human capital theory asserts that individuals invest in human capital in order to maximize their net wealth. Becker employed the investment framework primarily to analyze educational attainment and the rate of return to education for individuals. Chiswick (1978a, 1979) extended Becker's human capital framework substantially through its application to studying labor market aspects of immigration. This modified human capital model has since been instrumental in analyzing the process of immigrant adjustment in the host-country labor market.

Chiswick (1978a) was the first to argue that, holding the years of schooling constant, the ability to convert schooling into earnings might differ between the foreign-born and the native-born. This argument implied that immigrants would be unable to transfer completely the human capital accumulated in their home country to the labor market of the destination country. To analyze this aspect of immigration, economists have used the phrase 'international transferability of skills.' International transferability of skills can be viewed as a function of the similarities of the labor markets in the home country and the host country, with schooling and language being two important indicators.

21

Schooling has two components – an origin-specific component and an internationally transferable component. The importance of these two components differs by the level and the type of educational attainment. The more general the skills acquired through schooling in the origin country, the greater the transferability to the destination country and hence the lesser the decline in value of skills upon migration. Moreover, countries that share the same language tend to exhibit similarities in the nature and quality of their schooling and on-the-job training. Therefore, using the criterion of English-speaking country versus non-English-speaking country as an index of transferability, immigrants from English-speaking countries would be expected to have more transferable skills than otherwise identical immigrants from other countries.

Another criterion used to study the role of language in the immigrant's labor market performance is to develop a measure of linguistic distance between the country-of-origin and the destination country's language, rather than relying only on an English/non-English origin dichotomy. Immigrants whose origin language is more distant from English tend to have a lower fluency rate in English (Chiswick and Miller, 1992) and would thus be expected to possess skills that have low transferability in the U.S. labor market.

Several studies (Chiswick and Miller, 1994; Khan, 1997; Duleep and Regets, 1999) have used the transferability of skills argument to explain why immigrants are more likely than natives to make human capital investments in the destination country, other variables the same. First, immigrants face a lower opportunity cost of investment because they lack destination-specific skills. Secondly, acquiring host-country skills increases the transferability of their skills, thereby increasing the returns to their previous human capital investments. In fact, Khan (1997) argues that international transferability of skills is the primary factor explaining the differentials in post-migration investment in education among different immigrant groups.

The human capital investment framework discussed above is appropriate for testing hypotheses related to different types of human capital investments like migration, schooling, and on-the-job training. This study uses the human capital framework for analyzing educational attainment and school enrollment. Within this framework, attention is focused on factors that affect the demand for schooling, particularly in the context of immigrants.

THEORY OF DEMAND FOR SCHOOLING

Becker (1967, reprinted 1993) developed a model of optimal schooling. The model's underlying assumption is that individuals face a demand schedule, which reflects the marginal rate of return on investments in schooling, and a supply schedule, which reflects the marginal interest cost of obtaining funds to finance the investment in schooling. Optimal investment occurs when the marginal rate of return on investment equals the marginal interest cost of funds. Becker also emphasized the importance of the individual's background in influencing marginal cost and benefit schedules, and hence their equilibrium accumulation and return to human capital.

Chiswick (1988) re-interpreted Becker's model in the broader context of racial and ethnic groups. Chiswick argued that group differences in investment in schooling might arise from either differences in demand conditions, or differences in supply conditions, or from their combination. While some groups possess a greater "taste" for schooling, perhaps determined by cultural and historical factors, other groups simply place a higher value on future consumption compared to current consumption. These groups are expected to face a lower supply curve since they can supply funds at a lower interest cost. Group differences in demand conditions are believed to arise from group differences in the productivity of schooling. Such differences in productivity either arise from greater efficiency in acquiring units of skill from a given amount of schooling, or from being more efficient in applying these skills in the labor market (Chiswick, 1988). Differences in productivity are believed to arise from differences in out-of-school human capital formation, and factors influencing the quality of schooling demanded by different ethnic groups. Chiswick further maintained that group differences in the productivity of schooling vary more than group differences in the supply of investment funds, which in turn implies a positive relationship between levels of schooling and rates of return from schooling.

Parental investment in their children's schooling is determined principally by four factors: parental education, family income, family size and composition, and mother's time (Becker and Lewis, 1973; Leibowitz, 1974; Haveman et al., 1991). Furthermore, when investing in their children, parents base their decisions on tradeoffs they choose to make between the number of children and the resources (both parental time and parental income) per child. Becker (1964) first emphasized the importance of the interaction between quantity and quality of children for understanding fertility behavior, developing a formal model to study the child 'quality-quantity' tradeoff.

In the context of immigrants, Chiswick (1988) postulates that parental investment in children may be strongly influenced by the ethnic group to which they belong. Different ethnic groups have different perceptions on family size (fertility) and female labor force participation. This fundamental difference leads to group differences in relative prices of child quality and quantity. The group for which the cost of quantity is relatively higher than the cost of quality will invest more in fewer higher quality children. Chiswick thus attributes racial and ethnic group differences in the parental investment in children primarily to these group differences. He asserts that if two groups initially differ only in the price of quantity relative to quality of children, the quantity-quality fertility model generates group differences in fertility, skill formation, and rates of return; and these differences are transmitted from generation to generation.

DEVELOPMENT OF HYPOTHESES

The main hypothesis that emerges from the preceding discussion is that the demand for schooling is determined by economic incentives. An increase in the costs associated with schooling will cause individuals to substitute away from education while an increase in the benefits from schooling will raise the demand for it. Based on above discussions, the theoretical demand for schooling equation for immigrants may be written as:

Schooling = f (Pre-immigration conditions, Post-migration experience, Parental education, Parental income, Family size, Mother's labor supply)

Pre-immigration conditions and post-migration experience play vital roles in immigrant schooling investment decisions because they affect the level and transferability of skills that immigrants bring with them. While pre-immigration conditions include age-at-immigration, country-of-origin, and pre-immigration educational attainment, post-migration experience is associated with immigrant duration in the destination country.

This study analyzes the demand for schooling for two distinct immigrant populations – adult immigrants and immigrant children. For adult immigrants, schooling acquisition refers to years of schooling completed, whereas for immigrant children, it means school enrollment patterns. In the context of the theoretical model formulated here, this distinction is significant since the relevance of the explanatory variables specified in the theoretical model changes with the population being studied.

For the foreign-born, total schooling has two components – schooling acquired before, and schooling acquired after migration, referred to as pre-immigration and post-immigration schooling, respectively. Hashmi (1987) and Borjas (1982) have examined post-migration investment in schooling by immigrants in the United States. While their studies represented important advances on the subject, a serious limitation of both the studies was the need to estimate years of schooling in the United States as a residual. Such a procedure is likely to impart a negative correlation between measured post-migration years of schooling and measured pre-migration schooling. The datasets used for this study do not provide direct information on the division between pre-immigration schooling and post-migration schooling either. Therefore, based on the assumption of continuous school attendance from age six, post-migration schooling would have to be calculated as total years of schooling minus age-at-migration (which is current age minus years since migration). Using this procedure to study post-migration schooling would not resolve any of the bias inherent in the existing studies of Hashmi and Borjas. Hence, this study focuses on total schooling, a relatively unexplored area, rather than on post-migration investment in schooling. Moreover, often people first decide on the total level of schooling they will attain, and then decide on the location of their schooling. Consequently, the decision between pre- versus post-migration schooling becomes an endogenous one, which further justifies our study of total schooling.

For adult immigrants, age-at-arrival affects the costs of and returns from human capital investment. First, the older the age-at-immigration, the higher the opportunity costs associated with schooling (due to investment in the origin country).[5] Second, the older the age-at-immigration, the shorter is the duration in the host country to receive benefits from investment in destination-specific skills. These factors make migration as well as investment in post-migration schooling more profitable for younger immigrants compared to older immigrants. This profitability in turn implies that the demand for schooling will fall with age, and holding age constant, with duration in the destination. Consequently, total schooling increases with age at a decreasing rate. While immigration at an early age is considered beneficial, recent evidence also points to a lower return to schooling for those immigrating in late teens compared to those immigrating at a slightly younger or older age. For both adult immigrants and immigrant children, country-of-origin affects the costs of, and returns from, human capital investment.

For adults, the most important cause of country-of-origin differences is the dominant language spoken in the source country. The smaller the "linguistic distance" between the destination language and the immigrant's native language, the lesser is the depreciation of the country-of-origin human capital in the destination labor market. Country-of-origin differences among adults and children also arise from differences in the propensity for return migration. The higher the propensity for return migration, the lower the incentive for immigrants to invest in education for themselves or their children that are destination specific. Moreover, immigrants from some countries tend to be more educated, and consequently have a high income and invest more in their children's schooling. On the other hand, less educated immigrants from certain countries have low income coupled with larger family size, and accordingly invest less in their children. Besides, immigrant groups differ in female labor force participation rates, consequently affecting their children's school enrollment rates, particularly among the early age groups.

In studying schooling acquisition for both adult immigrants as well as for immigrant children, pre-immigration educational attainment is also relevant. Immigrants with a higher level of pre-immigration education tend to be more proficient in acquiring other forms of human capital, including language capital. In general, the more educated immigrants are expected to be more successful economically, more knowledgeable about quality of schooling in the destination country, and are more likely to invest in quality rather than quantity of children. For adult immigrants, the relation (substitute or complement) between pre-immigration and post-immigration schooling, together with their demand for schooling, determines the total level of schooling attained in the destination country.[6]

Post-migration experience measured by duration in the destination is a particularly important index of the economic adjustment of immigrants. Whether or not an immigrant invests in destination-specific schooling depends on some of the factors discussed earlier. However, if post-migration investments are made, they occur in the first few years after immigration and diminish thereafter (Hashmi, 1987). This arises because of three reasons. One, investments that are profitable tend to yield greater returns the earlier they are made. Two, the sooner such investments are made, the lower the opportunity cost of time since earnings rise with length of stay. Lastly, a delay in investment results in a shorter remainder working life in which to receive benefits from the investment. This investment pattern implies that the total level of schooling attained increases (albeit at a decreasing rate) with an increased duration in the destination, but that current enrollment rates decrease with duration.

Based on the theoretical model discussed above, the following hypotheses have been developed:

The model of immigrant adjustment based on human capital theory suggests that the economic status of immigrants improves with their duration of stay, i.e., immigrant assimilation in the host country is positively related to length of stay. The assimilation literature focuses on the length of time that it takes first-generation immigrants to achieve earnings parity with the native-born, and duration of residence in the destination country has a strong positive effect on immigrant assimilation in the host country. Implicit in the concept of 'assimilation' is the impact of immigrant generation, if we further distinguish between native-born who have foreign-born parents (second-generation immigrants) and native-born who have native-born parents (native-parentage). Second-generation immigrants will likely out-achieve first-generation immigrants because the former possess destination-specific skills. Second-generation immigrants may out-achieve native-parentage immigrants due to the positive influence of foreign-born parents arising from the selectivity bias in migration, which implies that immigrants tend to be disproportionately high ability or highly motivated people (Chiswick, 1977; Borjas, 1987).

Hypothesis 1: Among immigrants, educational attainment and school enrollment rates will differ by immigrant generation. The second-

generation of immigrants (children-of-immigrants) will exhibit higher educational attainment and school enrollment than the first-generation and may receive more schooling than those with native-born parents.

Language is an important component affecting transferability of skills since the lower the immigrant's fluency in the destination language, the higher the depreciation of his origin-specific skills in the destination, and the lower the transferability of the origin country skills. Furthermore, the lower an immigrant's transferability of skills, the greater the incentive to invest in destination-specific capital because of the positive effect that destination country's education has on the transferability of origin-country skills.

Hypothesis 2: *Among immigrants, educational attainment and school enrollment rates differ by country-of-origin. Immigrants to the U.S. from non-English-speaking countries will exhibit a higher demand for investments specific to the U.S., but will be handicapped by their lesser proficiency in English.*

Age-at-immigration affects labor market outcomes both directly and indirectly. The direct impact of age-at-immigration on labor market outcomes is easily explained in terms of costs and benefits. A higher age-at-immigration is associated with a higher opportunity cost of schooling/labor market experience (due to previous investment) coupled with a shorter remaining working life in the destination labor market to receive benefits. The direct impact of age-at-immigration is due to schooling and labor market experience in the source country not being recognized as equivalent to schooling in the host country. The indirect impact of age-at-immigration stems from the fact that younger immigrants are more able to adjust to linguistic and cultural challenges associated with migrating to a new country. For example, children have a superior ability to acquire new language skills, and this diminishes with age. Moreover, the complementarities between destination language and other forms of human capital (schooling) also suggest that youth will accrue more benefits from undertaking any destination-specific investment. In light of these effects, we can expect post-migration schooling[7] (a component of total schooling) to fall with age-at-immigration. Moreover, the negative effect of age is likely to be more pronounced for older immigrants, thus signifying a non-linear relation between age-at-immigration and post-migration schooling.

Hypothesis 3: *Educational attainment and school enrollment will vary with age-at-immigration. Specifically, post-migration educational attainment will fall with age-at-immigration, and fall at a decreasing rate. The effect of age-at-immigration on school enrollment rates will likely vary with the age group being studied.*

Based on the discussion that skills are not perfectly transferable, it is reasonable to assume that the foreign-born as a group have weaker labor market skills relative to the native-born. In terms of the transferability of skills argument, this difference translates to the foreign-born receiving a higher payoff from investment in U.S. schooling as compared to the native-born.

Hypothesis 4: *Immigrants will differ from natives in their educational attainment and school enrollment rates, exhibiting higher total educational attainment and higher school enrollment rates compared to natives of the same age, education, and other characteristics.*

While some of the hypotheses developed in this study were derived directly from the theoretical model of immigrant education, the other hypotheses were developed from the model based on the assumption of imperfect transferability of human capital between the origin-country and the host-country.

CHAPTER 4

Econometric Modeling of Immigrant Education

The estimating equations used to test the hypotheses developed for any empirical study are guided largely by the variables that are available in datasets used for the statistical analysis. The empirical analysis discussed in this study utilizes two datasets, namely, the 1990 U.S. Census of Population and Housing; and the October 1995 Current Population Survey.

1990 CENSUS OF POPULATION AND HOUSING

The Census survey questions follow a common rubric: a set of basic demographic questions (race, age, marital status) is asked of the entire U.S. population (the short-form questionnaire) and a more detailed set of social and economic questions (nativity, income, educational attainment, enrollment status) is asked of a subset of the full U.S. population (the long-form questionnaire).

The data from the Census are available as Public Use Microdata Samples (PUMS), which contain records for a sample of housing units with information on the characteristics of each unit and the people who inhabit it. Each PUMS is a stratified sample of the population, a sub-sample of the full census sample (approximately 15.9% of all housing units) that received long-form questionnaires. The 1990 data consists of three distinct microdata samples: the 5% (A) sample, the 1% (B) sample, and the 3% (O) sample. The households represented in each of the three samples are mutually exclusive.

The "A" and "B" samples have the same subject content but differ in their geographic coding. The "A" (5%) sample identifies every state, and most individual counties with 100,000 or more inhabitants. The "B" (1%) sample identifies metropolitan areas with 100,000 or more inhabitants individually and it groups together remaining metropolitan areas. The "O" sample has the same geographic composition as the "A" sample, but includes only those housing units with at least one person over age 60. The "A" and "O" samples each contain five percent of the population, or approximately one-third of the households that received the long-form questionnaire. The "B" sample contains one percent, i.e., one household for every one hundred households in the nation receiving the long-form questionnaire.

Since reliability improves with increases in sample size, the choice of sample size represents a balance between the level of precision desired and the resources available for working with microdata files. This study focuses on the schooling acquisition of U.S. immigrants from all countries-of-origin, hence the 1% microdata sample was the most appropriate. Had the focus of the study been on a specific foreign-born group (e.g., Asians or Hispanics), the much larger 5% sample would be necessary to ensure sufficient sample size by category.

Questions Related to Education

The 1990 Census asks questions pertaining to educational level and school enrollment of all persons aged three years and older. The questions used for defining the dependent variables (educational attainment and school enrollment) are as follows:

1. What is the highest level of schooling completed or highest degree received by the person? 17 response categories exist: No school completed, Nursery school, Kindergarten, Grades 1 to 4, Grades 5 to 8, five categories related to high school, four categories related to college, and finally three categories for graduate level education.

2. At any time since February 1, 1990, has the person attended regular school or college? 3 response categories exist: 1 = not enrolled in school, 2 = enrolled in public school, 3 = enrolled in private school.

For this study, the variable for total number of years of schooling was recoded as a continuous variable (EDUCATTN) and each response category was assigned the actual number of years of schooling it reflects. For example, completion of high school meant 12 years of education, completion of bachelor degree meant 16 years of education and so forth. The school enrollment variable was recoded as a dichotomous variable (ENROLLMT), where ENROLLMT = 0 if the person was not enrolled in school and ENROLLMT = 1 if the person was enrolled in either a public or private school.

Foreign-born and Pooled Sample Characteristics

The total sample size of the 1990 1% PUMS was 2,500,052. For this study, people living in group-quarters were excluded, so the sample size was reduced to 2,474,980. Educational attainment was analyzed for the adult population (those between 25 and 64 years of age) and school enrollment was analyzed for the youth population (those between 3 and 18 years of age). Therefore, the sample sizes are discussed separately for the two different analyses.

Educational attainment: The study of educational attainment was conducted for all adults between 25 and 64 years. The relevant sample size was 1,260,299. The population studied was either the foreign-born, the native-born, or the pooled sample of the foreign-born and native-born. The 'foreign-born' was defined as those born outside the United States. The 'native-born' was defined as those born in the United States. People born in U.S. outlying areas such as Puerto Rico (and similar areas over which the U.S. exercises jurisdiction), as well as people born at sea or of American parents living abroad, were excluded from this analysis. The size of the foreign-born sample was 115,839 and that of the native-born sample was 1,130,098. The pooled sample size was thus 1,245,937. Since the census does not ask the respondent their parents' place of birth, the study of the effects of immigrant generation on educational attainment for the adult population under consideration was not possible.

School Enrollment: The study of school enrollment was conducted for all children between 3 and 18 years of age.[8] The relevant sample size was 522,630. However, the absence in the child's file of important parental information, such as parental place of birth, parental education, and parental labor force participation, necessitated creating a child-parent link file. The Census provides data for all persons living in a sampled household, and since children under 18 years of age mostly live with their parents, their records are expected to be grouped with their parents' records within a single household. A dataset linking parental information (parental place of birth, parental education and labor-force participation) to each child record was created based on the information on the relationship of the respondent to the household head. The nature of the reported Census data did not permit identification of parents of those children living with grandparents (these children were less than 1% of the full sample), or those living with others who were not their parents, thus excluding them from this analysis. Furthermore, we had no information on the absent parent in case of single parent families, so observations with either parent missing were dropped. Our sample size thus reduced to 403,998 and this analysis was limited to two-parent households.[9]

The populations studied were first-generation immigrant children, second-generation immigrant children, and native-parentage children. 'First-generation' immigrant children ("child immigrants") were defined as those born outside the United States. 'Second-generation' immigrant children ("children of immigrants") were defined as those born in the U.S. but having one or both foreign-born parents. 'Native-parentage' children were defined as those born in the U.S. of U.S.-born parents. Children born in U.S. outlying areas such as Puerto Rico (and similar areas over which the United States exercises jurisdiction) as well as children born of American parents living abroad were excluded from this analysis. Also excluded in the definition of the generation variables were children who have both parents born in U.S. outlying areas. The size of the first-generation sample was 14,153, that of the second-generation sample 40,151, and the size of the native-born sample was 348,551. Therefore, the pooled sample size was 402,855.

OCTOBER CURRENT POPULATION SURVEY (CPS)

The Current Population Survey (CPS) is a monthly survey of about 57,000 households conducted by the Bureau of the Census for the Bureau of Labor Statistics. Respondents are interviewed to obtain information about the employment status of each member of the household 15 years of age and older. Each household is interviewed once a month for four consecutive months one year, and again for the corresponding time period a year later. Each month new households are added and old ones are dropped and thus part of the sample is changed. The CPS sample is scientifically selected on the basis of area of residence to represent the nation as whole, individual states, and other specified areas. The unit of observation in the CPS is the household, but the data are collected on each household member.

The basic CPS provides information on employment, unemployment, earnings, hours of work, and other labor force indicators on all household members above 16 years old. Such data are available by a variety of demographic characteristics including age, sex, race, marital status, and educational attainment. In addition to the basic demographic and labor force questions, questions on selected topics (school enrollment, income, employee benefits, and work schedules) are included as supplements to the regular CPS questionnaire in various monthly surveys. These supplemental topics are usually repeated in the same month each year. The October CPS supplement focuses on school enrollment. In addition to the basic CPS questions, the October CPS asks supplementary questions about school enrollment for all household members aged 3 years and above. Moreover, information on immigrant year of entry to the United States and information on a respondent's parental place of birth is vital to this study. Only the post-1994 CPS surveys provide this information and only the 1995 October CPS survey provides data on a respondent's English language skills. This study used October 1995 because it allowed examination of the relationship between school enrollment, immigration, and English language ability.

Questions Related to Education

The 1995 basic CPS asked questions pertaining to educational level to all persons 15 years and older. The October 1995 supplement asked questions on school enrollment to all persons 3 years and older. The questions used for defining the dependent variables (educational attainment and school enrollment) are as follows:

1. What is the highest level of school completed or the highest degree received by the person? Sixteen response categories exist: less than 1st grade, grades 1 to 4, two categories for middle school, five categories for high school, four categories for college, and three categories for graduate school.

2. a) Is the person attending or enrolled in nursery school, kindergarten, or elementary school? (asked of children between 3 and 5 years.) b) Is the person attending or enrolled in regular school? (asked separately of two different samples, one consisting of children between 6 and 14 years, the other consisting of adults 15 years and older.) Two

response categories exist: 1 = enrolled in school and 2 = not enrolled in school.

The total number of years of schooling variable was recoded as a continuous variable (EDUCATTN) and each response category was assigned the actual number of years of schooling it reflects. The school enrollment variable was recoded individually for each of the three different age groups. But in all three cases (i = age group 3 to 5, age group 6 to 14, age group 15 and above), the school enrollment variable was defined as a dichotomous variable (ENROLLMTi), where ENROLLMTi = 0 if the person was not enrolled in school and ENROLLMTi = 1 if the person was enrolled in either a public school or a private school.

Foreign-Born and Pooled Sample Characteristics

The total sample size of the 1995 CPS was 148,392. For this study, the non-interviewed records from the sample were excluded, reducing the sample size to 134,946 individuals. The analysis conducted using the CPS data was parallel to the Census data analysis. Moreover, the similarity in the variables available from the Census and the CPS enabled us to define the various sub-samples analogously.

Educational attainment: The study of educational attainment was conducted for all adults between 25 and 64 years. The relevant sample size was 69,746. Unlike the census analysis for adults, the 1995 CPS asks each respondent for their parental place of birth, thereby enabling us to study the effects of immigrant generation on educational attainment. The population studied was first-generation immigrant adults, second-generation immigrant adults, and native-parentage adults. 'First-generation immigrant adults' were defined as those adults born outside the United States who immigrated either as children or as adults. 'Second-generation immigrant adults' were defined as those adults born in the U.S., but having one or both foreign-born parents. 'Native-parentage adults' were defined as those adults born in the U.S. of U.S.-born parents. Adults born in U.S. outlying areas such as Puerto Rico (and similar areas over which the U.S. exercises jurisdiction) as well as adults born of American parents living abroad were excluded from this analysis. Also excluded were adults who have both parents born in U.S. outlying areas. The size of the first-generation adult sample was 7,496; that of the second-generation adult sample 4,506, and native-parentage adult sample 56,483. Therefore, the pooled sample size was 68,485. The data on period of immigration are for when the person first came to the United States to stay. The visa under which the respondent came or the motive for migration are not known. It is therefore not possible to identify those first-generation immigrants who entered the United States on student visas.

School Enrollment: The study of school enrollment was conducted for all children between 3 and 18 years of age. The relevant sample size was 29,289. The CPS file provides the parental place of birth for each record, allowing school enrollment by immigrant generations to be readily analyzed. However, the absence of two important explanatory variables, parental education and parental labor force participation, necessitated creating a child-parent link file. The CPS provides data for all persons living in a sampled household, and records of children less than 18 years are expected to be grouped with parents' records within a single household. For this study, a dataset linking parental information (parental education and parental labor-force participation) to each child record was created based on the information on the relationship of the respondent to the household head. The nature of the reported CPS data did not permit identification of parents of those children living with grandparents (these children were less than 1% of the full sample), or other adults who were not their parents, thereby excluding them from this analysis. Furthermore, we had no information on parental education and parental labor force participation for the missing parent in single-parent families, so we dropped observations with either parent missing. Our sample size thus reduced to 22,082 and this analysis was restricted to two-parent households.

The population studied was either first-generation children, or second-generation children, or native-born children. 'First-generation immigrant children' were defined as those born outside the United States. 'Second-generation immigrant children' were defined as those born in the U.S. but having one or both foreign-born parents. 'Native-parentage children' were defined as those born in the U.S. of U.S.-born parents. Children born in U.S. outlying areas, such as Puerto Rico (and similar areas over which the United States exercises jurisdiction), as well as children born abroad of American parents were excluded from this analysis. Also excluded were children who have both parents born in U.S. outlying areas. The size of the first-generation sample was 811;

that of the second-generation sample 2,870, and the native-parentage sample 18,355. Therefore, the pooled sample size was 22,036.

It should be noted that when defining the generation variables in both the Census and the CPS, foreign-born people were essentially considered 'first-generation' immigrants and native-born people were categorized into 'second-generation' immigrants or 'native-parentage' depending on their parental place of birth.

METHODOLOGY

In this study, two dependent variables, educational attainment and school enrollment, were estimated. Because educational attainment, which measures the total years of schooling, is a continuous variable, a multiple regression model was used for its estimation. In regression analysis, an estimating equation is developed to study the relationship between one variable called the explained, or dependent, variable and one or more other variables called independent, or explanatory, variables. A multiple regression model was considered where a dependent variable, Y, is predicted by a linear combination of several explanatory variables X_1, X_2, $X_3,....,$ X_k. The model to be estimated thus takes the form

$$Yi = \beta_0 + \beta_1 X_{1i} + \beta_2 X_{2i} + \beta_3 X_{3i} + ...+ \beta_k X_{ki} + e_i$$
$$i = 1,....,n$$

In this model, the unknown parameters, $\beta_1,....,\beta_k$, are the objects of estimation. The most common method of estimating the parameters of this linear regression model is Ordinary Least Squares (OLS), which uses the principle of least squares to maximize the explanatory power of the model. OLS will fit the β parameters in the equation for the observations i $=1,2,....,n$ by choosing values of the unknown parameters (β) such that the residual sum of squares (Σe_i^2) is minimized. The β parameters are referred to as the partial regression coefficients and reflect the (partial) effect of one explanatory variable on the mean value of the dependent variable when the values of other explanatory variables included in the model are held constant.

School enrollment, which measures the current enrollment status, is a binary variable, making the application of the linear regression model more complex, and making the binary choice model the appropriate choice. In the case of school enrollment, "not enrolled" is equated with zero and "enrolled" with one. These are qualitative choices and the zero/one coding is simply for convenience. Binary choice models assume that individuals are faced with a choice between two alternatives, and that the choice depends on identifiable characteristics. While parental education can be expected to be a primary determinant of enrollment outcomes, the exact enrollment choice made by each individual cannot be determined. Therefore, the approach used in analyzing binary choice models is to predict the likelihood that an individual will be "enrolled" in school.

In the linear probability model, which uses a binary variable as the dependent variable in a linear regression model, the predicted value of the binary dependent variable is the probability that the characteristic being studied (i.e. whether enrolled in school) occurs given the values of the independent variables. However, a major weakness of the linear probability model is that it does not constrain the predicted value to lie between 0 and 1. Given the problems associated with the linear probability model, transformation of the original model is necessary to produce predictions that lie in the (0,1) interval for all X. Use of a cumulative probability function solves this requirement. In particular, the probit model uses cumulative normal probability distribution to transform the original model providing a constrained version of the linear probability model.

This study relies on the following empirical specification of the probit model, in which the latent variable Y_i^* is expressed as the observed discrete outcome

$ENROLLMT_i = 1$ if $Y_i^* > 0$
$\qquad\qquad\quad = 0$ otherwise

where, $Y_i^* = \alpha + \beta X + e_i$

$ENROLLMT_i = 1$ if individual i enrolled
$\qquad\qquad\quad = 0$ otherwise

X = vector of explanatory variables such as age, parental education, and parental income that are believed to explain ENROLLMT.

β = set of parameters that reflect the impact of changes in X on the probability of enrollment, and are to be estimated by probit

e_i = standard error term

The response probability of enrollment is $P_i = $ Prob $(ENROLLMT = 1|X)$, which equals Prob $(Y^* > 0 |X)$. The latent variable formulation implies that we are interested in the effects of each X_j on Y^*. The probability P_i resulting from the probit model is interpreted as an estimate of the conditional probability that an individual will enroll in school, given a particular value of X. However, the parameters of the model (i.e., the magnitude of each β_j), like those of any nonlinear regression model, are not necessarily the marginal effects. We need to estimate the effect of X_j on the probability of success, i.e. Prob (ENROLLMT=1|X). The marginal effects vary with the values of X, and hence are usually calculated at the means of the regressors.

ESTIMATING EQUATIONS

The estimating equations for the two dependent variables, educational attainment and school enrollment, are discussed below. The definitions of the explanatory variables are included in Table 29, Appendix.

Educational Attainment Equation

The explanatory variables in the educational attainment estimating equation were of the following types: human capital variables (age, years since immigration), control variables (marital status, South, rural, black, Hispanic, and male), and country-of-origin variables.

The basic estimating equation for educational attainment was written as:

Educational attainment = f (H, L, D, G, C)

H is a vector of human capital variables, including age and age-at-immigration. *Age* is expected to have a positive impact on educational attainment. To test the rate of increase of educational attainment with age, age squared was introduced into the estimating equation.[10] *Age-at-immigration* (AGEIMMIG) captures the impact of immigration at different ages. There are three concepts of age important in the context of the foreign-born: current age of an immigrant, age at the time of immigration, and years since migration. The three age variables are, however, collinear – therefore, given any two of them in the regression or probit, the effect of the third can be calculated.

For ease of interpretation, this study used the variables, AGE, AGE^2, and AGEIMMIG, $AGEIMMIG^2$. As an immigrant's length of stay in the U.S (YSM) increases, his stock of investment in U.S. schooling increases but at a decreasing rate. Therefore, holding age constant, as age-at-immigration increases, educational attainment is expected to fall but at a decreasing rate. Furthermore, following Schaafsma and Sweetman's (2001) decomposition of age-at-immigration into several age-at-immigration classes, in an immigrant earnings analysis for Canada, this study incorporates eight age-at-immigration dummy variables (*e.g.*, age-at-immigration = 0 to 4, 5 to 12, and so on) to capture the differing effects of immigrating over particular age ranges.

L represents language skills measured by linguistic distance. The exact causal process between educational attainment and English language fluency has often been debated; hence, immigrant language fluency is not an appropriate variable to use in the estimating equation for educational attainment. *Linguistic distance*, which measures the distance between the immigrant's mother tongue and English, is more relevant, as it is exogenous to the schooling decision. This study uses an index of 'linguistic distance' developed by Chiswick and Miller (1998), based on a set of language learning scores (LS). The scores were originally developed by Hart-Gonzalez and Lindemann (1993) (see Table 30, Appendix) based on the degree of difficulty that English speakers have learning foreign languages. A low linguistic score indicates a high level of difficulty (e.g., Japanese LS = 1.00) and a high score indicates a low level of difficulty (e.g., French LS = 2.50). The linguistic scores simply imply that there is a greater linguistic distance between English and Japanese than there is between English and French. Based on the assumption of linguistic symmetry (it is as difficult for A-speakers to learn language B, as it is for B-speakers to learn language A), Chiswick and Miller (1998) incorporated linguistic scores into a model of language fluency to measure the effects of linguistic distance on an immigrant's English fluency. For purposes of empirical research, linguistic distance is measured as the reciprocal of the linguistic score. A higher value of LD thus implies a greater distance between English and the origin language.

D is a vector of demographic control variables for gender, marital status, and race/ethnicity. Dichotomous variables *black* and *Hispanic* were used to measure the impact of racial disadvantage on educational attainment, *male* was used to control for gender differentials on educational attainment, *married* captures the effect of being married as distinct from other marital statuses.

G is a vector of geographic variables. Dichotomous variables, *south*, representing south/non-south residence, and *rural*, representing urban/rural residence, controls for the effect of region of residence and urbanization on educational attainment, respectively.

C is a vector of country-of-origin dummy variables to capture country fixed effects, including the impact of the transferability of skills and motive for migration. Based on the assumption that economic migrants from English-speaking, developed countries possess highly transferable skills, the benchmark group created for the country-of-origin analysis was English-speaking, developed countries. Other countries were clustered into broad groups to represent economic migrants from certain major non-English-speaking countries and also refugee migrants from other countries.

When applying the estimating equation to the pooled sample of native-born and foreign-born, native-born was the benchmark in the C vector, so a dichotomous variable for the English-speaking countries was added to the equation.

School Enrollment Equation

Since most states in the United States have mandatory school attendance laws at the elementary and secondary levels, enrollment rates among children aged 6 and 15 is close to 100 percent. A frequency distribution of school enrollment by age using the 1990 Census data revealed that enrollment rates are around 97 percent for children between 6 and 15 years of age. The 3 percent not enrolled include those children receiving home-schooling. The enrollment rate drops to 95 percent for 16-year-olds, to 92 percent for 17-year-olds, and to 79 percent for 18-year-olds. There also exists a wide variation in the enrollment rates of children below 5 years: 19 percent for 3-year-olds, 39 percent for 4-year-olds, and 68 percent for 5-year-olds.

A frequency distribution of school enrollment rates by age using the 1995 October CPS data also depicts the same enrollment pattern. For children between 6 and 15 years, the enrollment rates are around 98 to 99 percent. The enrollment rate drops to 97 percent for 16-year-olds, to 95 percent for 17-year-olds, and to 76 percent for 18-year-olds. There also exists a wide variation in the enrollment rates of children below 5 years: 37 percent for 3-year-olds, 62 percent for 4-year-olds, and 94 percent for 5-year-olds.

Given the pattern of school attendance rates of the 6-15 age group, this study analyzes school enrollment for only the two extreme age groups: 3 to 5-year-olds (preschoolers) and 16 to 18-year-olds (high school teenagers). However, the reasons for non-enrollment among preschoolers are usually very different from non-enrollment in high school among teenagers. A primary deterrent of enrollment in preschool is family income since most nursery schools are private. Teenagers, on the other hand, choose to drop out of high school without a diploma because of economic, social, and other factors. In general, factors like racial/ethnic differences or mother's labor force participation also have different impacts on the enrollment behavior of a preschooler versus a high school teenager. Therefore, our econometric analysis on school enrollment is conducted separately for the 3 to 5 age group and the 16 to 18 age group.

The explanatory variables in the school enrollment estimating equation were of the following types: human capital variables (age, years since immigration), demographic control variables (south, rural, black, Hispanic, and male), family variables (parental education, parental income, family size, mother's labor force participation) and country-of-origin variables.

The basic estimating equation for school enrollment was written as:
School Enrollment $= f$ **(H, D, G, F, C)**

H is a vector of human capital variables including *age* and *age-at-immigration*. The impact of age on the probability of school enrollment depends on the age group being analyzed. It is reasonable to expect enrollment to rise with age if we are looking at a sample of children below five years. At the same time, the probability of enrollment drops in the late-teen years. To test the relation between school enrollment and age, dichotomous age variables were introduced into the estimating equation. *Age-at-immigration* (AGEIMIG) captures the impact of immigration at different ages. When analyzing the 3 to 5 age group, we introduced one age-at-immigration dummy variable to capture the effect of immigration prior to, versus immigration after, age 2 years. In the 16 to 18 age group study, we used three age-at-immigration dummy variables to reflect the effects of migrating between 0 and 4 years, between 5 and 12 years, and after 13 years of age. The school enrollment equation also uses *English proficiency* as a measure of immigrant children's language skills.

D is a vector of demographic control variables for gender and race/ethnicity. Dichotomous variables for being *black* and *Hispanic* were used to measure the racial disadvantage on preschool and on high school enrollment. *Male* was used to control for gender differentials in preschool and high school enrollment.

G is a vector of geographic variables. Dichotomous variables, *south*, representing south/non-south residence, and *rural*, representing urban/rural residence, control for the effect of region of residence and urbanization on preschool and high school enrollment.

F is a vector of family variables. *Mother's education, father's education, and family income* are expected to positively impact school enrollment rates. High school students may work part-time or full-time for several reasons. Since being employed (and hence having own earned income) has a negative effect on enrollment, we account for this negative bias by subtracting teenager's own earned income from total family income. Both *family size* and *mother's labor supply* serve as proxies for both time investment that a parent makes in a child and other similar parental investments, hence their importance in the school enrollment equation.

C is a vector of country-of-origin variables. In the enrollment equation, their purpose is to capture broad ethnic group variations in family characteristics and other country-of-origin fixed effects. However, the classification scheme remains the same as used in the educational attainment equation. The English-speaking countries are the benchmark when the analysis is limited to the foreign-born.

When applying the estimating equation to the pooled sample of native-born and foreign-born, native-born was the benchmark in the C vector, so a dichotomous variable for the English-speaking countries was added to the equation.

CHAPTER 5

Educational Attainment of Adult Immigrants

This chapter is an empirical study of the largely ignored issue of the determinants of educational attainment among adult immigrants. Using current population survey (CPS) data, differences in educational attainment are analyzed by immigrant generation (first, second, and higher order generations), and among the foreign-born by country of birth and age-at-immigration. The analysis is repeated using 1990 census data to test if the results are robust. However, due to data constraints, the census study does not permit the immigrant generation analysis.

EMPIRICAL ANALYSIS OF THE 1990 CENSUS DATA

The pooled sample of foreign-born and native-born adults enables us to do a comparative analysis of educational attainment among the native-born and the foreign-born. The foreign-born sample allows us to study educational attainment by different countries-of-origin and different ages-at-immigration. Furthermore, separate regressions on the native-born and the foreign-born populations allow a comparative study of the determinants of educational attainment between the two groups.

Educational Attainment of Native-Born and Foreign-Born Adults

This section discusses the results for the pooled sample of 1,245,937 foreign-born and native-born adults between 25 and 64-years-old. Comparative statistics for adult (25 to 64-year-olds) immigrants and

TABLE 1. MEANS AND STANDARD DEVIATIONS OF VARIABLES, FOREIGN-BORN AND NATIVE-BORN ADULTS, UNITED STATES, 1990

	Foreign-Born		Native-Born	
Variable	Mean	S.D.	Mean	S.D.
Educational attainment	11.70	4.41	13.19	2.65
Male	0.49	0.50	0.49	0.50
Age	40.63	10.86	41.43	11.15
Black	0.08	0.27	0.11	0.32
Hispanic	0.40	0.49	0.04	0.19
Married	0.72	0.45	0.68	0.47
South	0.24	0.42	0.35	0.48
Rural	0.06	0.24	0.27	0.44
Age-at-immigration	24.62	11.19	n.a.	n.a.
Linguistic distance	0.50	0.16	n.a.	n.a.
Sample size	115,839		1,130,098	

Source: 1990 Census of Population of United States, Public Use Microdata Sample, 1% file.

Note: Variables are as defined in Table 29 in Appendix.
    n.a. = Variable not applicable.

natives are summarized in Table 1. An average immigrant is 41 years of age, has 11.7 years of schooling, and has been in the United States for about 16 years. The average native is also 41 years, but has a higher education level (13.2 years) than the average immigrant. Furthermore, the native-born are more southern and more rural than the foreign-born. While 6% of immigrants live in rural areas and 24% live in the South, about 27% of natives live in rural areas and 35% live in the South. An important point to note is the large percentage of Hispanics in the foreign-born sample.[11]

Ordinary Least Squares regression results for the pooled sample are summarized in Table 2. The dependent variable for the regression equation was years of schooling, referred to as 'educational attainment.' Four different specifications were considered. The primary explanatory variables used in all four specifications were male, age, age squared, black, Hispanic, married, South, rural, foreign-born, age-at-immigration, and age-at-immigration squared. The basic specification (column 1 in table 2) was a simple model, which used the above mentioned set of demographic and geographic variables as the explanatory variables. The second specification (column 2 in table 2) introduced the 'Linguistic Distance' variable to the set of explanatory variables. The third specification (column 3 in table 2) added birthplace dummy variables to the set of explanatory variables in column 1. The last specification (column 4 in table 2) deleted the quadratic age-at-immigration variables but added age-at-immigration dummy variables as regressors.

Focusing on model (1) of the regression for total pooled population (column 1 in table 2), the positive sign of age coupled with the negative sign of age squared reflects that education increases with age at a decreasing rate. The peak occurs at 30.5 years, after which the effect of age on education becomes negative. The age variable captures two effects: one, the cohort effect, which implies that younger cohorts acquire more education, and two, the life cycle effect, which implies that education increases with age in the life cycle within a cohort. Apparently, beyond age 30.5 years, the negative cohort effect dominates the positive life cycle effect.

The effect of foreign birth on educational attainment (irrespective of the country-of-origin) is given jointly by the coefficients of the variable 'foreign-born' and the variables on 'age-at-immigration.'[12] Evaluated for different values of age-at-immigration, the partial effect of foreign birth on educational attainment is: 0.27 for age-at-immigration=1, 0.02 for age-at-immigration=5, -0.28 for age-at-immigration=10, -0.80 for age-at-immigration=20, and -1.21 for age-at-immigration=30. This pattern indicates that as age-at-immigration increases, the differential in educational attainment between the foreign-born and the native-born increases. Moreover, the sign and magnitude of the calculated partial effect implies that while foreign-born adults migrating before the age of 5 acquire more schooling than the native- born, those migrating after the age of 5 acquire lesser schooling than the native-born.

TABLE 2. REGRESSION ESTIMATES OF POOLED SAMPLE OF FOREIGN-BORN AND NATIVE-BORN ADULTS, UNITED STATES, 1990

DEPENDENT VARIABLE: EDUCATIONAL ATTAINMENT

Variable	(1)	(2)	(3)[a]	(4)[b]
Constant	10.597 (277.36)	10.573 (276.76)	10.605 (282.70)	10.652 (278.30)
Male	0.143 (29.50)	0.143 (29.64)	0.160 (33.70)	0.143 (29.56)
Age	0.183 (99.86)	0.184 (100.24)	0.180 (100.12)	0.181 (98.30)
Age^2	-0.003 (122.45)	-0.003 (122.66)	-0.003 (123.15)	-0.003 (120.95)
Black	-1.029 (119.93)	-1.014 (118.18)	-1.036 (122.05)	-1.027 (119.83)
Hispanic	-2.528 (240.58)	-2.406 (196.75)	-1.637 (128.14)	-2.499 (237.48)
Married	0.313 (57.14)	0.310 (56.90)	0.324 (60.47)	0.312 (57.32)
South	-0.285 (55.07)	-0.284 (54.79)	-0.303 (59.36)	-0.286 (55.26)
Rural	-1.065 (200.86)	-1.059 (199.78)	-1.034 (198.54)	-1.063 (200.74)
Foreign-born	0.340 (11.06)	0.344 (10.91)	n.e.	n.e.
Age-at-immigration (Ageimmig)	-0.067 (28.96)	-0.072 (31.43)	-0.075 (32.47)	n.e.
Ageimmig)^2/100	0.051 (11.99)	0.054 (13.04)	0.036 (8.66)	n.e.
Linguistic distance * Non-English	n.e.	1.864 (35.60)	n.e.	n.e.
Non-English	n.e.	-0.900 (31.65)	n.e.	n.e.
BIRTHPLACE				
English-speaking countries	n.e.	n.e.	1.630 (44.83)	n.e.
Africa	n.e.	n.e.	3.097 (47.61)	n.e.
Mexico	n.e.	n.e.	-2.599 (72.58)	n.e.
Cuba	n.e.	n.e.	1.600 (33.05)	n.e.
S. & C. America	n.e.	n.e.	0.955 (23.84)	n.e.
Caribbean	n.e.	n.e.	0.156 (2.77)	n.e.
Southern Europe	n.e.	n.e.	-1.429 (33.89)	n.e.

TABLE 2 (continued)

Variable	(1)	(2)	(3)[a]	(4)[b]
E. & C. Europe	n.e.	n.e.	1.467 (39.70)	n.e.
N. & W. Europe	n.e.	n.e.	1.346 (18.74)	n.e.
Philippines	n.e.	n.e.	2.273 (48.81)	n.e.
China	n.e.	n.e.	0.507 (9.13)	n.e.
Vietnam	n.e.	n.e.	-0.471 (8.27)	n.e.
East Asia	n.e.	n.e.	2.098 (46.97)	n.e.
South Asia	n.e.	n.e.	3.020 (57.73)	n.e.
Middle East	n.e.	n.e.	1.630 (30.66)	n.e.
Other Asia	n.e.	n.e.	-0.673 (12.28)	n.e.
Remaining countries	n.e.	n.e.	0.098 (1.97)	n.e.
AGE-AT-IMMIGRATION				
0 to 4	n.e.	n.e.	n.e.	0.503 (14.06)
5 to 12	n.e.	n.e.	n.e.	0.121 (4.44)
13 to 19	n.e.	n.e.	n.e.	-1.241 (62.26)
20 to 24	n.e.	n.e.	n.e.	-1.052 (58.46)
25 to 29	n.e.	n.e.	n.e.	-0.781 (42.72)
30 to 34	n.e.	n.e.	n.e.	-1.086 (45.70)
35 to 44	n.e.	n.e.	n.e.	-1.501 (63.54)
45 to 64	n.e.	n.e.	n.e.	-2.005 (57.34)
Adjusted R^2	0.134	0.134	0.166	0.135
Sample size	1,245,937	1,245,937	1,245,937	1,245,937

Source: 1990 Census of Population of United States, Public Use Microdata Sample, 1% file.

Note: Variables are as defined in Table 29 in Appendix.

    n.a. = Variable not applicable.

    t statistics are in parentheses.

    [a] and [b] benchmark group is all native-born adults.

The remaining coefficients in the estimating equation are all highly significant. Men acquire 0.15 years more education than women. Being black reduces educational attainment by 1.03 years, and being Hispanic decreases educational attainment by 2.53 years. Residence in the southern states or in the rural areas has a negative impact on educational attainment. Being married is associated with 0.31 more years of education.

The linguistic distance variable (LD) was added to the set of explanatory variables in Table 2, column 2. Since linguistic distance is a relevant explanatory variable only for immigrants from non-English-speaking countries, a non-English dummy variable (which equals 1 if an adult is from a non-English-speaking country, 0 otherwise) is also introduced in specification 2. The same non-English dummy variable is interacted with LD. The partial effect of linguistic distance on educational attainment is obtained jointly from the coefficient of the LD and non-English interaction term and the coefficient of the non-English dummy variable.[13] The partial effect of the linguistic distance variable is 0.96. This indicates a differential of 64 percentage points in educational attainment between the non-English-speaking group with the largest linguistic distance from English (LS = 1 and LD = 1) and the non-English-speaking group with the smallest linguistic distance from English (LS = 3.0 and LD = 0.33). Inclusion of linguistic distance into the model has only a limited impact on the coefficients of the original estimating equation.

The third specification (column 3 of table 2) included the usual explanatory variables (excluding LD) plus the country variables representing different countries-of-origin. The benchmark was native-born adults, hence, holding all other coefficients constant, the coefficients represent the difference in education between foreign-born adults from a particular country and all native-born adults. The coefficients indicate that Africans acquire 3.1 years more education, South Asians 3 years more, Filipinos 2.3 years more, and East Asians 2.1 years more education compared to native-born adults. Cubans, South and Central Americans, all Europeans (except Southern Europe), Middle Easterners, and immigrants from English-speaking countries acquire between 1 and 1.6 years more education compared to native-born adults. The positive differential is negligible for immigrants from China and the Caribbean.

Immigrants from Mexico, Southern Europe, Vietnam, and Other Asia have lower levels of educational attainment compared to native-borns. The differential is greatest for Mexicans (2.6 years), followed by Southern Europeans (1.4 years), and Vietnamese (0.5 years). The inclusion of the country-of-origin variables is associated with a change in the estimated impact of the variable Hispanic. For Hispanic, the partial effect changes from −2.53 to −1.64. Since Mexico is the largest source country for Hispanic immigrants, it is not surprising that part of the negative effect of being Hispanic on educational attainment is captured by the large negative coefficient of Mexico.[14]

Specification 4 (column 4 in table 2) included the usual explanatory variables (without the age-at-immigration quadratic variables) plus the age-at-immigration dummy variables. The benchmark was native-born adults, hence, holding other coefficients constant, the coefficients give the difference in education between foreign-born people from a particular age-at-immigration group and native-born adults. Our analysis indicates that adults immigrating in the 0 to 4 age group acquire 0.5 years more education, and those immigrating in the 5 to 12 age group acquire 0.1 year more education compared to native-born adults. Compared to native-born adults, those migrating between 25 and 29 acquire 0.78 fewer years of education, while those immigrating between 13 and 19, and between 20 and 24, acquire about 1.1 fewer years of education. For foreign-born adults immigrating after age 30, the differential with their native counterparts gets progressively larger (*i.e.* the 45 to 64 age group has a higher differential than the 35 to 44 group, and the 35 to 44 group has a higher differential than the 30 to 34 group).

The quadratic specification on age-at-immigration simply depicted a negative relation between age-at-immigration and educational attainment. When plotted graphically, this relationship appears as a smooth downward sloping curve (Figure 2A). The specification with the age-at-immigration dummy variables clearly portrays a more detailed picture. When educational attainment is plotted graphically (Figure 2B) against the age-at-immigration dummy variables, we observe a dip in age-at-immigration at 13 to 19 years and a local peak in age-at-immigration at 25 to 29 years. The age-at-immigration dichotomous variables indicate that educational attainment decreases with an increase in age-at-immigration. But it captures an additional effect not obvious from the quadratic specification results; that is, immigrating during the secondary school years is associated with a

Figure 2. Effect of Age-at-Immigration on Educational Attainment

A.   Quadratic Specification of Age-at-Immigration Variable

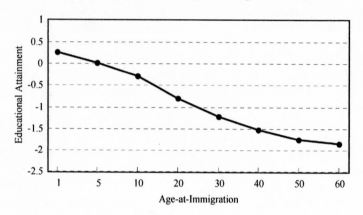

B.   Categorical Specification of Age-at-Immigration Variable

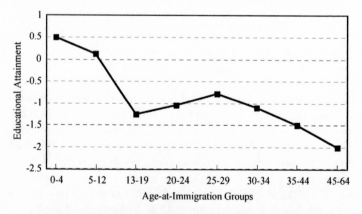

Both graphs A and B are based on the 1990 Census data and display educational attainment on the Y-axis. A depicts age-at-immigration as a continuous variable on the X-axis. The data is obtained from column 1 of Table 2. B depicts age-at-immigration as a categorical variable on the X-axis. The data is obtained from column 4 of Table 2 where age-at-immigration is separated into categorical dummy variables.

greater disadvantage than if the immigration took place a few years earlier or later.

Educational Attainment of Foreign-Born Adults

This section discusses the results for the sample of 115,389 foreign-born adults between 25 and 64-years-old. Table 3 presents the means and standard deviations of educational attainment, age-at-immigration, and linguistic distance by country-of-origin. As column 1 in the table indicates, approximately 11% of immigrants are from English-speaking countries (United Kingdom, England, Australia, New Zealand, British West Indies). The dominant immigrant source country is Mexico (21%), followed by South and Central America (11%), East and Central Europe (10%), Southern Europe and East Asia (6%), and the Philippines (5%). The remaining country groups constitute 2 to 4% each. Column 2 in the table indicates that immigrants from South Asia and Africa have the largest investment in schooling (15 years), followed by those from East Asia, the Middle East, and the Philippines (14 years), East and Central Europe, North and West Europe, and English-speaking countries (13 years), and China, Vietnam, and Cuba (12 years). Immigrants from Mexico have the lowest level of education (8 years), followed by those from the Caribbean, Southern Europe, and Other Asia (11 years).

LD is defined as the reciprocal of the linguistic score, where a high score implies a small distance from English. We thus expect individuals with small language scores (large linguistic distance) to have high values of LD, while individuals with large language scores (small linguistic distance) to have LD close to zero. Column 3 in Table 3 indicates that the mean values of LD are highest for East Asia, followed by China and Vietnam, and the mean values of LD are lowest for North and West Europe. This seems reasonable to expect since languages spoken in East Asia, such as Japanese and Korean, are considered the most distant from English, while those spoken in North and West Europe, such as French and Spanish, are much closer to English. The mean values of age-at-immigration (column 4 in Table 3) by country-of-origin group reflects that immigrants from Europe, the English-speaking countries, and Mexico tend to migrate at a much earlier age (22 years) compared to those from Africa, South and Central America, and the Middle East (26 years), and those from East and South Asia, China, and Vietnam (28 years).

TABLE 3. SUMMARY STATISTICS BY COUNTRY-OF-ORIGIN, FOREIGN-BORN ADULTS, UNITED STATES, 1990

Country-of-Origin	Sample Size	Educational Attainment	Linguistic Distance	Age-at-Immigration
English-speaking countries	12,578 (10.86)[a]	13.32 (2.84)[b]	n.a.	22.57 (11.68)
Africa	2,182 (1.88)	14.73 (3.14)	0.48 (0.11)	26.04 (8.59)
Mexico	24,804 (21.41)	8.09 (4.24)	0.44 (0.002)	22.43 (9.93)
Cuba	4,894 (4.22)	11.81 (3.89)	0.44 (0.01)	24.09 (13.36)
S. & C. America	13,043 (11.26)	11.49 (4.07)	0.44 (0.02)	26.04 (10.36)
Caribbean	3,267 (2.82)	10.65 (4.05)	0.43 (0.02)	26.15 (10.50)
Southern Europe	6,972 (6.02)	10.61 (4.22)	0.45 (0.07)	21.64 (11.12)
E. & C. Europe	11,046 (9.54)	13.42 (3.07)	0.45 (0.04)	22.21 (12.63)
N. & W. Europe	1,590 (1.37)	13.37 (3.72)	0.39 (0.05)	21.54 (11.25)
Philippines	5,923 (5.11)	14.14 (2.91)	0.50 (0.04)	27.83 (10.84)
China	3,349 (2.89)	12.17 (4.93)	0.80 (0.04)	30.71 (11.96)
Vietnam	3,163 (2.73)	11.53 (4.164	0.69 (0.06)	28.36 (10.33)
East Asia	7,235 (6.25)	14.09 (3.21)	0.94 (0.11)	28.30 (10.11)
South Asia	4,185 (3.61)	15.05 (3.54)	0.57 (0.04)	28.27 (9.20)
Middle East	3,686 (3.18)	13.74 (3.76)	0.56 (0.08)	25.79 (10.91)
Other Asia	3,448 (2.98)	11.39 (5.09)	0.67 (0.13)	26.32 (10.36)
Remaining countries	4,474 (3.86)	11.31 (4.23)	0.50 (0.12)	24.93 (11.52)
Total	115,839 (100.00)	11.70 (4.41)	0.50 (0.16)	24.63 (11.19)

Source: 1990 Census of Population of United States, Public Use Microdata Sample, 1% file.

Note: Variables are as defined in Table 29 in Appendix.

    n.a. = Variable not applicable.

    [a] denotes percent foreign-born in column 2.

    [b] standard errors for all variables are indicated in parentheses

Table 4 presents the means and standard deviations of educational attainment by different age-at-immigration groups. We see that immigrants who migrate prior to their teenage years have schooling levels very similar to the native-born. While native-borns have a mean schooling level of 13.1 years, those immigrating between 0 and 4 years acquire an average of 13.5 years of schooling, with the 5 to 12 group following very closely at 12.8 years. The 13 to 19 group attains an average of 11.2 years of schooling, which is lower than any group immigrating between 20 and 34. Moreover, those migrating between 25 and 29 have a slightly higher average (12.0 years) compared to the age group prior to (11.6 years) or the age group after (11.7 years) them.

TABLE 4. SUMMARY STATISTICS OF EDUCATIONAL ATTAINMENT BY AGE-AT-IMMIGRATION, FOREIGN-BORN ADULTS, UNITED STATES, 1990

Age-at-Immigration	Sample Size	Educational Attainment
0 to 4	5,738 (4.95)[a]	13.45 (2.93)[b]
5 to 12	10,005 (8.64)	12.80 (3.30)
13 to 19	19,861 (17.15)	11.26 (4.15)
20 to 24	24,223 (20.91)	11.66 (4.33)
25 to 29	23,006 (19.86)	12.01 (4.54)
30 to 34	13,363 (11.53)	11.72 (4.67)
35 to 44	13,565 (11.71)	11.05 (4.88)
45 to 64	6,078 (5.25)	10.05 (5.03)
Total	115,839 (100.00)	11.70 (4.41)

Source: 1990 Census of Population of United States, Public Use Microdata Sample, 1% file.

Note: Variables are as defined in Table 29 in Appendix.
   [a] denotes percent in age-at-immigration group.
   [b] standard errors are indicated in parentheses.

Ordinary Least Squares regression results for the foreign-born sample are summarized in Table 5. The dependent variable for the regression equation was years of schooling, referred to as 'educational attainment.' Corresponding to specification 1, 2, 3, and 4 of the pooled sample, four different specifications were considered for the foreign-born sample. The basic specification (column 1 of Table 5) indicates that educational attainment increases with age but at a decreasing rate. In the case of the foreign-born population, the peak is reached at a later age (37 years) compared to 30.5 years in the case of the pooled sample. The negative sign of age-at-immigration together with the positive sign of age-at-immigration squared implies that as age at immigration increases, educational attainment falls, but at a decreasing rate. Evaluated for different values of age-at-immigration, the partial effect of age-at-immigration on educational attainment is: -0.06 for age-at-immigration=1, -0.06 for age-at-immigration=10, -0.05 for age-at immigration =20, -0.05 for age-at-immigration=30, and -0.04 for age-at-immigration=50. The remaining coefficients in the estimating equation are all highly significant. Foreign-born men acquire about 0.47 years more schooling compared to foreign-born women. Residence in southern states increases educational attainment by 0.58 years while rural residence decreases educational attainment by 0.89 years.

Introducing linguistic distance into the specification (column 2) did not produce a significant impact on any of the other coefficients in the estimating equation. The partial effect of the linguistic distance variable is 0.03.[15] This indicates a differential of 3 percentage points in educational attainment between the foreign-born adults with the largest linguistic distance from English (LS = 1 and LD = 1) and the foreign-born adults with the smallest linguistic distance from English (LS = 3.0 and LD = 0.33).

The next specification (column 3 in Table 5) introduced the country-of-origin regressors to the basic set of explanatory variables.[16] In analyzing the foreign-born sample, the benchmark group was the English-speaking foreign countries. Therefore, holding all other coefficients constant, the coefficient of the country variables is interpreted as the difference in years of schooling between foreign-born people from a particular country group and foreign-born people from English-speaking countries. Immigrants from Africa, the Philippines, East and South Asia, and the Middle East show higher levels of educational attainment than those from the English-speaking countries. While Africa and South Asia are ahead of English-speaking countries by 1.5 years, the other three groups share a differential of less than one year. South and Central America, the Caribbean, Vietnam, Southern Europe, and Mexico show lower levels of educational attainment than English-speaking countries. Mexicans indicate the largest differential (4.1 year), followed by Southern Europe and Other Asia (2.5 years), Vietnam and the Caribbean (2 years), and South and Central America (1 year). The inclusion of the country-of-origin variables results in a change in the estimated impact of the variable Hispanic. The differential for Hispanic goes down from –3.89 to –1.67, perhaps because part of the negative effect is captured by the large negative coefficient of Mexico.

Specification 4 (column 4 in table 5) excludes the country dummy variables and LD, but includes the usual explanatory plus the age-at-immigration dummy variables. In analyzing the foreign-born sample, the benchmark age-at-immigration group was the 25 to 29 group. Our analysis indicates that adults who immigrated between the ages of 0 to 4 acquired 1.2 more years of schooling, and those who migrated between age 5 and 12 acquired 0.9 more years of schooling compared to the benchmark group—those who immigrated between the ages of 25 and 29. Adults immigrating in the 13 to 19 and 20 to 24 age groups and those who immigrated at age 30 and older have less schooling than the 25 to 29 group. The differential is less than one half of a year except for the oldest group (age 45 to 64 at immigration). In summary, the 13 to 19 group and the 20 to 24 group acquire lower education compared to the 25 to 29 age group, as do immigrants with older age at arrival. Moreover, the total years of schooling decline progressively in relation to the benchmark group for those immigrating after age 34.

Regressions estimated separately for the foreign-born and native-born adults are presented in Table 6. The coefficients of the native-born sample regression are very similar to the pooled sample regression coefficients because native-borns constitute 91% of the total pooled sample. All the coefficients are highly significant. Two interesting points to note when the regressions are estimated separately are as follows: one, the educational attainment differential between Hispanics and non-Hispanics is more pronounced for the foreign-born (3.9 years) compared to the native-born (1.6 years); two, the educational attainment differential between blacks and non-blacks is more pronounced for the native-born (1.1 years) compared to the foreign-born (0.3 years).

**TABLE 5. REGRESSION ESTIMATES OF FOREIGN-BORN ADULTS,
UNITED STATES, 1990**

DEPENDENT VARIABLE: EDUCATIONAL ATTAINMENT

Variable	(1)	(2)	(3)[a]	(4)[b]
Constant	11.939	12.21	13.047	11.365
	(64.17)	(64.62)	(73.94)	(58.06)
Male	0.471	0.483	0.599	0.468
	(20.11)	(20.62)	(27.33)	(20.02)
Age	0.148	0.150	0.118	0.125
	(16.27)	(16.43)	(13.84)	(13.38)
Age^2	-0.002	-0.002	-0.002	-0.002
	(20.47)	(20.52)	(18.31)	(17.81)
Black	-0.255	-0.283	-0.409	-0.247
	(5.29)	(5.63)	(7.73)	(5.13)
Hispanic	-3.885	-3.678	-1.669	-3.837
	(157.38)	(128.58)	(29.98)	(155.13)
Married	-0.058	-0.058	0.075	-0.048
	(2.14)	(2.15)	(2.96)	(1.80)
South	0.583	0.574	0.217	0.571
	(21.12)	(20.82)	(8.21)	(20.74)
Rural	-0.890	-0.908	-0.623	-0.874
	(20.67)	(21.03)	(15.37)	(20.35)
Age-at-immigration	-0.058	-0.058	-0.068	n.e.
(Ageimmig)	(16.60)	(16.73)	(20.98)	
$Ageimmig^2/100$	0.028	0.026	0.023	n.e.
	(4.39)	(4.04)	(3.92)	
Linguistic distance * Non-English	n.e.	1.001	n.e.	n.e.
		(10.86)		
Non-English	n.e.	-0.969	n.e.	n.e.
		(14.91)		
BIRTHPLACE				
Africa	n.e.	n.e.	1.256	n.e.
			(14.42)	
Mexico	n.e.	n.e.	-4.092	n.e.
			(60.87)	
Cuba	n.e.	n.e.	-0.098	n.e.
			(1.18)	
S. & C. America	n.e.	n.e.	-0.552	n.e.
			(8.31)	
Caribbean	n.e.	n.e.	-1.643	n.e.
			(19.72)	
Southern Europe	n.e.	n.e.	-2.812	n.e.
			(49.38)	
E. & C. Europe	n.e.	n.e.	0.026	n.e.
			(0.53)	

TABLE 5 (continued)

Variable	(1)	(2)	(3)[a]	(4)[b]
N. & W. Europe	n.e.	n.e.	0.114 (1.15)	n.e.
Philippines	n.e.	n.e.	0.928 (15.35)	n.e.
China	n.e.	n.e.	-0.859 (11.60)	n.e.
Vietnam	n.e.	n.e.	-1.946 (25.62)	n.e.
East Asia	n.e.	n.e.	0.715 (12.50)	n.e.
South Asia	n.e.	n.e.	1.564 (22.86)	n.e.
Middle East	n.e.	n.e.	0.159 (2.23)	n.e.
Other Asia	n.e.	n.e.	-2.086 (28.52)	n.e.
Remaining countries	n.e.	n.e.	-1.452 (20.99)	n.e.
AGE-AT-IMMIGRATION				
0 to 4	n.e.	n.e.	n.e.	1.182 (20.00)
5 to 12	n.e.	n.e.	n.e.	0.895 (18.75)
13 to 19	n.e.	n.e.	n.e.	-0.316 (8.12)
20 to 24	n.e.	n.e.	n.e.	-0.207 (5.62)
30 to 34	n.e.	n.e.	n.e.	-0.275 (6.31)
35 to 44	n.e.	n.e.	n.e.	-0.693 (15.64)
45 to 64	n.e.	n.e.	n.e.	-1.286 (20.99)
Adjusted R^2	0.198	0.198	0.305	0.202
Sample size	115,839	115,839	115,839	115,839

Source: 1990 Census of Population of United States, Public Use Microdata Sample, 1% file.

Note: Variables are as defined in Table 29 in Appendix.
    n.e. = Variable not entered. t statistics are in parentheses.
    [a] benchmark group is all foreign-born adults from English-speaking countries.
    [b] benchmark group is all foreign-born adults who immigrated between ages 25 and 29.

TABLE 6. REGRESSION ESTIMATES OF FOREIGN-BORN AND NATIVE-BORN ADULTS, UNITED STATES, 1990

DEPENDENT VARIABLE: EDUCATIONAL ATTAINMENT

Variable	Foreign-Born	Native-Born
Constant	11.939 (64.17)	10.496 (281.63)
Male	0.471 (20.11)	0.115 (24.44)
Age	0.148 (16.27)	0.187 (104.45)
Age^2	-0.002 (20.47)	-0.003 (127.72)
Black	-0.255 (5.29)	-1.060 (128.02)
Hispanic	-3.885 (157.38)	-1.619 (126.65)
Married	-0.058 (2.14)	0.347 (65.26)
South	0.583 (21.12)	-0.340 (67.75)
Rural	-0.890 (20.67)	-1.049 (208.71)
Age-at-immigration (Ageimmig)	-0.058 (16.60)	n.e.
$Ageimmig^2/100$	0.028 (4.39)	n.e.
Adjusted R^2	0.198	0.104
Sample size	115,839	1,130,098

Source: 1990 Census of Population of United States, Public Use Microdata Sample, 1% file.

Note: Variables are as defined in Table 29 in Appendix.
   n.e. = Variable not entered.
   t statistics are in parentheses.

The summary statistics discussed in Table 1 indicate that 40% of the foreign-born sample is Hispanic. To test if the Hispanic pool dominates the results derived from our earlier analysis of the foreign-born sample, the basic specification (only demographic and geographic variables) and the specification with age-at-immigration dummies were run separately on the Hispanic sample and the non-Hispanic sample (see Table 32, Appendix). The coefficients that differ in their relevance in explaining educational attainment among the Hispanics and non-Hispanics are male, black, and age-at-immigration. Contrary to the total foreign-born sample and the non-Hispanic sample, male Hispanics have a lower education relative to their female counterparts. While being black increased educational attainment by 1.3 years among Hispanics, being black reduced educational attainment by 0.7 years among non-Hispanics. The black/non-black differential in schooling attainment between the Hispanic and non-Hispanic is perhaps explained by the fact that black Hispanics originate primarily from the Caribbean or Central America, and not from Mexico. The difference in the age-at-immigration effects is evident from the sign and magnitude of the continuous age-at-immigration variable, as well as the discrete age-at-immigration dummy variables. The Hispanic sample reflects that educational attainment falls with age-at-immigration at an increasing rate, but for the non-Hispanic sample educational attainment increases with age-at-immigration at a decreasing rate. The analysis by age-at-immigration shows that the positive effect of immigrating in the preteen years is strongest for Hispanics. This probably reflects the common practice of teenage Mexicans migrating to the United States to seek employment, and/or the practice of many Mexican families to not emphasize the enrollment of their teenage children in high school soon after migration.

EMPIRICAL ANALYSIS OF THE OCTOBER 1995 CPS DATA

The CPS data enable us to analyze educational attainment by immigrant generation for all adults. Therefore, in this case, the pooled sample of first-generation, second-generation, and native-parentage adults allows us to do a comparative analysis of educational attainment among the three generations. Secondly, separate regressions by immigrant generation allow a comparative study of the determinants of educational attainment between the three groups. Lastly, the first-generation sample allows us to study educational attainment by different countries-of-origin and by different ages-at-immigration.

Educational Attainment of First-Generation, Second-Generation, and Native-Parentage Adults

This section discusses the results for the pooled sample of 68,485 first-generation, second-generation, and native-parentage adults between 25 and 64-years-old. Comparative statistics for all adult (25-64-year-olds) natives, and first- and second-generation immigrants are summarized in Table 7. An average first-generation immigrant is 41 years of age, has

TABLE 7. MEANS AND STANDARD DEVIATIONS OF VARIABLES, FIRST-GENERATION, SECOND-GENERATION, AND NATIVE-PARENTAGE ADULTS, UNITED STATES, 1995

Variable	First-Generation	Second-Generation	Native-Parentage
Educational attainment	11.81	13.68	13.46
	(4.24)	(2.67)	(2.44)
Male	0.49	0.50	0.49
	(0.50)	(0.50)	(0.50)
Age	40.85	44.46	41.71
	(10.65)	(11.95)	(10.54)
Black	0.07	0.02	0.13
	(0.26)	(0.14)	(0.34)
Hispanic	0.47	0.20	0.03
	(0.50)	(0.40)	(0.16)
Married	0.72	0.67	0.67
	(0.45)	(0.47)	(0.47)
South	0.24	0.23	0.38
	(0.43)	(0.42)	(0.48)
Non-MSA	0.05	0.11	0.22
	(0.22)	(0.31)	(0.42)
Age-at-immigration	24.79	n.a.	n.a.
	(11.07)		
Sample size	7,496	4,506	56,483

Source: October 1995 Current Population Survey, United States Census Bureau.

Note: Variables are as defined in Table 29 in Appendix.
    n.a. = Variable not applicable.
    standard errors for all variables are in parentheses.

11.8 years of schooling, and has been in the United States for about 16 years. The average second-generation immigrant is 45 years of age, and has an education level (13.7 years) similar to an average first-generation immigrant or native-parentage adult (13.5 years). Furthermore, the natives are more southern (38%) than either the first-generation or second-generation (24% each). Compared to 22% of native-born adults living in non-metropolitan areas, only 11% of second-generation immigrants and fewer (5%) first-generation immigrants live in non- metropolitan areas. The first-generation has a large percentage of Hispanics (47%) compared to the second-generation (20%) and native-parentage (3%) adults.

Ordinary Least Square regression results for the pooled sample are summarized in Table 8. The dependent variable for the regression equation was years of schooling, referred to as 'educational attainment.' Three different specifications were considered. The primary explanatory variables used in all three specifications were male, age, age squared, black, Hispanic, married, South, non-MSA, age-at-immigration and age-at-immigration squared. The variable non-MSA was used in place of rural since there was no information on urban/rural in the CPS. The basic specification (column 1 in table 8) was a simple model, which used the above-mentioned set of demographic and geographic variables as the explanatory variables along with the two immigrant generation variables. The second specification (column 2 in table 8) added birthplace dummy variables to the set of explanatory variables. The last specification (column 3 in table 8) deleted the quadratic age-at-immigration variables but added age-at-immigration dummy variables as regressors.

Focusing on model (1) of the regression for the total pooled population, the positive sign of age coupled with the negative sign of age squared shows an increase in education with age but at a decreasing rate. The peak occurs at 32.5 years, after which the effect of age on education becomes negative. The age variable captures two effects – one, the cohort effect, which implies that younger cohorts acquire more education, and two, the life cycle effect, which implies that education increases with age in the life cycle within a cohort. Beyond a certain point (in this case, 32.5 years), the negative cohort effect dominates the positive life cycle effect.

The negative and positive coefficients of age-at-immigration and age-at-immigration squared, respectively, indicate that educational

TABLE 8. REGRESSION ESTIMATES OF POOLED SAMPLE OF FIRST-GENERATION, SECOND-GENERATION, AND NATIVE-PARENTAGE ADULTS, UNITED STATES, 1995

DEPENDENT VARIABLE: EDUCATIONAL ATTAINMENT

Variable	(1)	(2)[a]	(3)[b]
Constant	11.408 (71.14)	11.500 (73.26)	11.49 (71.55)
Male	0.136 (6.91)	0.149 (7.74)	0.137 (6.98)
Age	0.136 (17.74)	0.129 (17.22)	0.131 (17.14)
Age^2	-0.002 (21.28)	-0.002 (20.82)	-0.002 (20.70)
Black	-0.689 (20.36)	-0.688 (20.56)	-0.688 (20.34)
Hispanic	-2.586 (59.16)	-1.317 (23.69)	-2.548 (58.21)
Married	0.306 (14.14)	0.322 (15.22)	0.306 (14.17)
South	0.278 (12.63)	-0.301 (13.94)	-0.280 (2.76)
Non-MSA	0.810 (34.60)	-0.795 (34.67)	-0.810 (34.62)
Age-at-immigration (Ageimmig)	-0.058 (6.53)	-0.068 (7.76)	n.e.
$Ageimig^2/100$	0.038 (2.45)	0.027 (1.75)	n.e.
First-generation	0.539 (4.48)	n.e.	n.e.
Second-generation	0.472 (11.63)	0.317 (7.95)	0.466 (11.49)
BIRTHPLACE			
English-speaking countries	n.e.	1.580 (11.06)	n.e.
Africa	n.e.	2.970 (10.35)	n.e.
Mexico	n.e.	-2.442 (17.46)	n.e.
Cuba	n.e.	1.339 (6.59)	n.e.
S. & C. America	n.e.	0.401 (2.62)	n.e.
Caribbean	n.e.	-0.261 (1.34)	n.e.

TABLE 8 (continued)

Variable	(1)	(2)[a]	(3)[b]
Southern Europe	n.e.	-1.387 (8.33)	n.e.
E. & C. Europe	n.e.	1.973 (13.67)	n.e.
N. & W. Europe	n.e.	3.262 (10.17)	n.e.
Philippines	n.e.	1.910 (11.29)	n.e.
China	n.e.	1.130 (5.72)	n.e.
Vietnam	n.e.	-0.387 (1.79)	n.e.
East Asia	n.e.	2.112 (11.73)	n.e.
South Asia	n.e.	3.371 (17.64)	n.e.
Middle East	n.e.	2.095 (9.51)	n.e.
Other Asia	n.e.	-0.153 (0.77)	n.e.
Remaining countries	n.e.	1.820 (11.29)	n.e.
AGE-AT-IMMIGRATION			
0 to 4	n.e.	n.e.	0.818 (5.54)
5 to 12	n.e.	n.e.	0.431 (4.11)
13 to 19	n.e.	n.e.	-0.960 (12.15)
20 to 24	n.e.	n.e.	-0.751 (11.31)
25 to 29	n.e.	n.e.	-0.401 (5.71)
30 to 34	n.e.	n.e.	-0.693 (8.30)
35 to 44	n.e.	n.e.	-1.039 (11.82)
45 to 64	n.e.	n.e.	-1.713 (13.55)
Adjusted R^2	0.110	0.149	0.112
Sample size	68,485	68,485	68,485

Source: October 1995 Current Population Survey, United States Census Bureau.

Note: Variables are as defined in Table 29 in Appendix.
    n.e. = Variable not entered. t statistics are in parentheses.
    [a] and [b] benchmark group is all native-born adults.

attainment decreases with age-at-immigration, and it decreases at a decreasing rate. Evaluated for different values of age-at-immigration, the partial effect of being a first-generation immigrant on educational attainment is: 0.52 for age-at-immigration=1, 0.23 for age-at-immigration=5, -0.01 for age-at-immigration=10, -0.47 for age-at-immigration=20, and -0.86 for age-at-immigration=30. Clearly, the effect of foreign-birth (being a first-generation immigrant) on educational attainment depends on age-at-immigration. Only those immigrating at a very early age will have attainment levels similar to their native counterparts. However, the positive coefficient of second-generation clearly indicates that second-generation immigrants acquire 0.47 years more total schooling than native-born adults.

The remaining coefficients in the estimating equation are all highly significant. Men attain 0.14 years more education than women. Being black reduces educational attainment by 0.69 years, and being Hispanic decreases educational attainment by 2.59 years. Residence in the southern states or in a non-metropolitan area is associated with a negative impact on educational attainment. Being married is associated with 0.31 more years of education.

The second specification (column 2 in Table 8) included the usual explanatory variables (without age-at-immigration quadratic variables) plus the country dummy variables representing all countries-of-origin. The benchmark was native-parentage adults, hence holding all other coefficients constant, the age-at-immigration coefficients represent the difference in education between first-generation immigrants from a particular country and native-parentage adults. The coefficients indicate that Africans, South Asians, and North and West Europeans acquire 3 years more education, and Filipinos, East Asians, East and Central Europeans, and Middle Easterners about 2 years compared to all native-born adults. Cubans, Chinese, and immigrants from English-speaking countries acquire between 1 and 1.5 years more education compared to native-parentage adults. The positive differential is negligible for immigrants from South and Central America.

Immigrants from Mexico and Southern Europe have lower levels of educational attainment compared to all native-born (second-generation and native-parentage). The differential is 2.5 years for Mexicans and 1.4 years for Southern Europeans. The inclusion of the country-of-origin variables is associated with a change in the estimated impact of the variable Hispanic. For Hispanic, the partial effect changes from –2.59 to –1.32. This change in the magnitude of the

Hispanic variable can be attributed to the large negative coefficient of Mexico.

Specification 3 (column 3 in table 8) included the usual explanatory variables plus the age-at-immigration dummy variables to represent different age groups at which immigrants migrated. The benchmark was all native-parentage adults, hence the coefficients give the difference in education between foreign-born people from a particular age-at-immigration group and all native-born adults. Our analysis indicates that adults immigrating in the 0 to 4 age group acquire 0.8 years more education, and those immigrating in the 5 to 12 age group acquire 0.4 years more education compared to the benchmark group. Also relative to all second-generation immigrants and native-parentage adults, first-generation immigrants migrating between 25 and 29 acquire 0.41 fewer years of education, while those immigrating between 13 and 19 acquire 1.03 fewer years of education, and those between 20 and 24 acquire about 0.8 years less of education. For foreign-born adults immigrating after age 30, the differential with their native and second-generation counterparts gets progressively larger with age (*i.e.* the 45 to 64 age group has a higher differential than the 35 to 44 group, and the 35 to 44 group has a higher differential than the 30 to 34 group).

As in the Census analysis, the quadratic specification on age-at-immigration using the CPS data simply depicted a negative relation between age-at-immigration and educational attainment. When plotted graphically, this relationship appears as a smooth downward slope curve (Figure 3A). The specification with the age-at-immigration dichotomous variables portrays a more detailed picture. When educational attainment is plotted graphically (Figure 3B) against the age-at-immigration dummy variables, we observe a dip in age-at-immigration at 13 to 19 years and a local peak at 25 to 29 years. The age-at-immigration dichotomous variables indicate that educational attainment falls with an increase in age-at-immigration. However, it also captures an additional effect not obvious from the quadratic specification results - immigrating in the teenage years has a negative effect on educational attainment relative to immigrating in the preteen years or the post-twenties.

Figure 3. Effect of Age-at-Immigration on Educational Attainment

A.   Quadratic Specification of Age-at-Immigration Variable

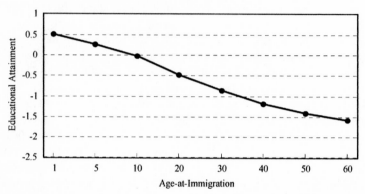

B.   Categorical Specification of Age-at-Immigration Variable

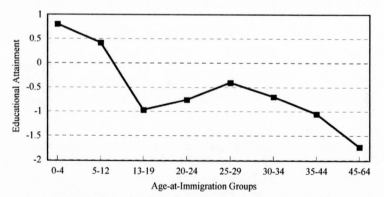

Both A and B are based on the 1995 CPS data and show educational attainment
on the Y-axis. A depicts age-at-immigration as a continuous variable on the X-
axis. The graph is obtained from column 1 of Table 8. B depicts age-at-
immigration as a categorical variable on the X-axis. The graph is obtained from
column 4 of Table 8 where age-at-immigration is separated into categorical
dummy variables.

Educational Attainment of First-Generation Adults

This section discusses the results for the sample of 7,496 first-generation adults between 25 and 64-years-old. Table 9 presents the means and standard deviations of educational attainment and age-at-immigration by country-of-origin. As column 1 in the table indicates, approximately 9% of immigrants are from English-speaking countries (United Kingdom, England, Australia, New Zealand, British West Indies). The dominant immigrant source country is Mexico (22%), followed by South and Central America (12%), East and Central Europe (9%), the Philippines (6%), and Southern Europe and East Asia (5%). The remaining country groups constitute 1 to 4% each.

Column 2 indicates that immigrants from South Asia, Africa, and North and West Europe have the largest investment in schooling (15 years), followed by those from East Asia, the Middle East, the Philippines, China, and East and Central Europe (14 years), North and West Europe, and English-speaking countries (13 years). Immigrants from Mexico have the lowest level of education (9 years), followed by those from Cuba, the Caribbean, Southern Europe, South and Central America, and Other Asia (11 years). The mean values of age-at-immigration (column 3) by country-of-origin group reflect that immigrants from Southern Europe, North and West Europe, Cuba, and Mexico tend to migrate at a much earlier age (20-24 years) compared to those from East Asia, Vietnam, and China (28-31 years). The other country groups lie in between the two extremes.

Table 10 presents the means and standard deviations of educational attainment by different age-at-immigration groups. Immigrants who migrate prior to their teenage years have schooling levels very close to the native-born. While native-borns have a mean schooling level of 13.5 years, those immigrating between 0 and 4 years acquire an average of 13.7 years of schooling, with the 5 to 12 group following very closely at 13 years. The 13 to 19 group attains an average of 11.2 years of schooling, which is lower than any group immigrating between 20 and 44. Moreover, those migrating between 25 and 29 have a slightly higher average (12.2 years) compared to the age group prior to (11.6 years) or the age group after (11.9 years) them. Educational attainment is lowest for those immigrating after age 45.

TABLE 9. SUMMARY STATISTICS BY COUNTRY-OF-ORIGIN, FIRST-GENERATION ADULTS, UNITED STATES, 1995

Country-of-Origin	Sample Size	Educational Attainment	Age-at-Immigration
English-speaking countries	720 (9.61)[a]	13.73 (2.68)[b]	23.70 (11.66)
Africa	94 (1.25)	14.98 (3.26)	26.66 (8.54)
Mexico	1650 (22.01)	8.66 (3.83)	22.79 (9.94)
Cuba	233 (3.11)	11.96 (3.35)	24.04 (13.10)
S. & C. America	890 (11.87)	11.58 (3.87)	25.54 (9.97)
Caribbean	287 (3.83)	11.06 (3.72)	26.44 (8.94)
Southern Europe	360 (4.80)	11.64 (4.16)	20.26 (11.16)
E. & C. Europe	698 (9.31)	14.10 (2.96)	27.22 (13.82)
N. & W. Europe	70 (0.93)	15.31 (2.31)	22.70 (8.74)
Philippines	438 (5.84)	14.11 (2.82)	26.78 (11.28)
China	259 (3.46)	13.60 (4.37)	30.61 (11.67)
Vietnam	191 (2.55)	11.99 (4.17)	29.18 (13.06)
East Asia	363 (4.84)	14.43 (2.64)	27.73 (10.42)
South Asia	307 (4.10)	15.57 (3.04)	26.74 (7.86)
Middle East	183 (2.44)	14.33 (3.62)	25.58 (10.14)
Other Asia	252 (3.36)	11.71 (4.52)	26.10 (10.42)
Remaining countries	501 (6.68)	13.97 (3.17)	25.87 (10.77)
Total	7,496 (100.00)	11.82 (4.23)	24.79 (11.07)

Source: October 1995 Current Population Survey, United States Census Bureau.

Note: Variables are as defined in Table 29 in Appendix.
      [a] denotes percent foreign-born in column 2.
      [b] standard errors of all variables are indicated in parentheses.

TABLE 10. SUMMARY STATISTICS OF EDUCATIONAL ATTAINMENT BY AGE-AT-IMMIGRATION, FIRST-GENERATION ADULTS, UNITED STATES, 1995

Age-at-Immigration	Sample Size	Educational Attainment
0 to 4	305	13.71
	(4.07)[a]	(2.69)[b]
5 to 12	620	13.04
	(8.27)	(3.08)
13 to 19	1172	11.19
	(15.64)	(3.96)
20 to 24	1656	11.55
	(22.09)	(4.15)
25 to 29	1436	12.15
	(19.16)	(4.43)
30 to 34	994	11.91
	(13.26)	(4.44)
35 to 44	889	11.52
	(11.86)	(4.62)
45 to 64	424	10.69
	(5.65)	(4.95)
Total	7,496	11.82
	(100.00)	(4.23)

Source: October 1995 Current Population Survey, United States Census Bureau.

Note: Variables are as defined in Table 29 in Appendix.
[a] denotes percent in age-at-immigration group.
[b] standard errors are indicated in parentheses.

Ordinary Least Squares regression results for the first-generation immigrant sample[17] are summarized in Table 11. Three different specifications corresponding to specification 1, 3, and 4 of the pooled sample are considered for the first-generation sample. The basic specification indicates that educational attainment increases with age until age 29, after which it starts declining due to younger cohorts receiving more schooling. The negative sign of age-at-immigration

TABLE 11. REGRESSION ESTIMATES OF FIRST-GENERATION ADULTS, UNITED STATES, 1995

DEPENDENT VARIABLE: EDUCATIONAL ATTAINMENT

Variable	(1)	(2)	(3)
Constant	12.97 (18.88)	14.37 (21.92)	12.78 (17.65)
Male	0.462 (5.43)	0.520 (6.54)	0.469 (5.53)
Age	0.111 (3.29)	0.062 (1.98)	0.075 (2.18)
Age^2	-0.002 (4.29)	-0.001 (3.19)	-0.001 (3.22)
Black	-0.328 (1.97)	-0.284 (1.59)	-0.317 (1.90)
Hispanic	-3.879 (42.99)	-1.086 (5.56)	-3.817 (42.21)
Married	0.043 (0.44)	0.162 (1.79)	0.048 (0.49)
South	0.312 (2.87)	0.033 (0.32)	0.287 (2.64)
Non-MSA	-0.700 (4.00)	-0.465 (2.83)	-0.702 (4.02)
Age-at-immigration (Ageimmig)	-0.053 (4.11)	-0.068 (5.56)	n.e.
Ageimmig^2/100	0.028 (1.19)	0.038 (1.74)	n.e.
BIRTHPLACE			
Africa	n.e.	1.223 (3.24)	n.e.
Mexico	n.e.	-4.217 (17.41)	n.e.
Cuba	n.e.	-0.498 (1.55)	n.e.
S. & C. America	n.e.	-1.320 (5.70)	n.e.
Caribbean	n.e.	-1.988 (7.65)	n.e.
Southern Europe	n.e.	-2.731 (11.88)	n.e.
E. & C. Europe	n.e.	0.589 (3.07)	n.e.

TABLE 11 (continued)

Variable	(1)	(2)	(3)
N. & W. Europe	n.e.	1.739 (4.04)	n.e.
Philippines	n.e.	0.497 (2.30)	n.e.
Vietnam	n.e.	-1.924 (6.70)	n.e.
East Asia	n.e.	0.654 (2.84)	n.e.
South Asia	n.e.	1.872 (7.68)	n.e.
Middle East	n.e.	0.586 (2.02)	n.e.
Other Asia	n.e.	-1.667 (6.44)	n.e.
Remaining countries	n.e.	0.281 (1.39)	n.e.
AGE-AT-IMMIGRATION			
0 to 4	n.e.	n.e.	1.119 (4.83)
5 to 12	n.e.	n.e.	0.826 (4.67)
13 to 19	n.e.	n.e.	-0.404 (2.77)
20 to 24	n.e.	n.e.	-0.306 (2.30)
30 to 34	n.e.	n.e.	-0.229 (1.50)
35 to 44	n.e.	n.e.	-0.605 (3.72)
45 to 64	n.e.	n.e.	-1.287 (5.82)
Adjusted R^2	0.215	0.322	0.218
Sample size	7,496	7,496	7,496

Source: October 1995 Current Population Survey, United States Census Bureau.

Note: Variables are as defined in Table 29 in Appendix.
n.e. = Variable not entered. t statistics are in parentheses.
[a] benchmark group is all foreign-born adults from English-speaking countries.
[b] benchmark group is all foreign-born adults who immigrated between ages 25 to 29.

together with the positive sign of age-at-immigration squared implies that as age-at-immigration increases, educational attainment falls but at a decreasing rate. Evaluated for different values of age-at-immigration, the partial effect of age-at-immigration on educational attainment is: -0.05 for age-at-immigration=1, -0.05 for age-at-immigration=10, -0.04 for age-at-immigration=20, -0.04 for age-at-immigration=30, and -0.03 for age-at-immigration=40. Not all the remaining coefficients are significant. Foreign-born men acquire about 0.46 years more in schooling compared to foreign-born women. Residence in southern states increases educational attainment by 0.31 years while a non-metropolitan residence decreases educational attainment by 0.70 years. Being Hispanic has a highly significant negative effect on educational attainment.

The next specification (column 2 in table 11) introduced the country-of-origin regressors. In analyzing the first-generation sample, the benchmark group was the English-speaking foreign countries. Therefore, the coefficient of the country variables is interpreted as the difference in years of schooling between first-generation immigrants from a particular country group and first-generation immigrants from English-speaking countries. Immigrants from Africa, the Philippines, East and South Asia, the Middle East, and Europe (except southern) show higher levels of educational attainment than those from the English-speaking countries. Immigrants from South and Central America, the Caribbean, Vietnam, Southern Europe, and Mexico show lower levels of educational attainment than English-speaking countries. Mexicans have the largest differential (4.2 years), followed by Southern Europe (3 years), and the remaining country groups have less than a one year differential. The differential for Hispanic goes down from a highly significant −3.88 to a much less significant −1.09, but the negative effect of Hispanic on educational attainment is clearly captured by the significant, large negative coefficient of Mexico.

The last specification (column 3 in table 11) includes the usual explanatory variables plus the age-at-immigration dummy variables to represent different age groups at which immigrants migrated. In analyzing the first-generation sample, the benchmark age-at-immigration group was the 25 to 29 group. Hence the coefficients give the difference in education between first-generation immigrants from a particular age-at-immigration group and first-generation immigrants who immigrated between 25 and 29 years of age. Our analysis indicates that adults who immigrated between the ages of 0 to 4 years acquire 1.1 more years of schooling, and those who migrated between the ages of 5 and 12 years acquire 0.8 more years of schooling compared to the benchmark group. Adults immigrating after 13 years of age but prior to 34 years of age acquire less education than the benchmark group but the differential is less than one half of a year. The total years of schooling declines progressively in relation to the benchmark group for those immigrating after age 34.

Comparative Study of First-Generation, Second-Generation, and Native-Parentage Adults

Regressions estimated separately for the first-generation immigrants, second-generation immigrants, and native-born adults are presented in Table 12. While educational attainment increases until age 37 and declines thereafter for both second-generation immigrants and native-parentage adults, first-generation immigrants reach their peak much earlier at age 28. One noteworthy factor is the variation in the Hispanic/non-Hispanic differential in educational attainment across the three groups of study. The Hispanic/non-Hispanic differential is most pronounced in the first-generation (3.9 years), followed by the second-generation (1.7 years), and the native-born (1.3 years).

In order to study the effect of foreign-parentage on educational attainment, we consider the sample of all native-born adults (i.e., second-generation and native-parentage adults). We introduced three variables (mother-only foreign-born, father-only foreign-born, and both parents foreign-born) into the basic regression specification. The benchmark is both parents being native-born. Our results indicate that having either parent foreign-born or both parents foreign-born has a positive effect on educational attainment. This result agrees with Schultz's (1984) finding that if both parents are foreign-born, duration of residence in the United States is associated with increased levels of schooling. Also if immigrants are favorably self-selected and more able (Borjas, 1987; Chiswick, 1977, 1999), it suggests that they are more inclined to invest in their children's schooling than native-born parents. Therefore, it is not surprising that second-generation immigrants (who by definition have at least one foreign-born parent) acquire more schooling than their native counterparts.

TABLE 12. REGRESSION ESTIMATES OF FIRST-GENERATION, SECOND-GENERATION, AND NATIVE-PARENTAGE ADULTS, UNITED STATES, 1995

DEPENDENT VARIABLE: EDUCATIONAL ATTAINMENT

Variable	First-Generation	Second-Generation	Native-Parentage	All Native-Born
Constant	12.97	11.775	11.35	11.32
	(18.88)	(19.93)	(69.54)	(72.03)
Male	0.462	0.250	0.091	0.103
	(5.43)	(3.32)	(4.56)	(5.34)
Age	0.111	0.136	0.136	0.137
	(3.29)	(4.94)	(17.43)	(18.34)
Age^2	-0.002	-0.002	-0.002	-0.002
	(4.29)	(6.45)	(20.55)	(21.79)
Black	-0.328	-0.365	-0.709	-0.707
	(1.97)	(1.29)	(21.55)	(21.58)
Hispanic	-3.879	-1.650	-1.254	-1.333
	(42.99)	(14.66)	(18.35)	(23.28)
Married	0.043	0.432	0.333	0.339
	(0.44)	(5.26)	(15.25)	(16.06)
South	0.312	-0.012	-0.343	-0.328
	(2.87)	(0.12)	(15.82)	(15.43)
MSA	-0.700	0.880	0.804	0.809
	(4.00)	(8.30)	(35.70)	(36.65)
Age-at-immigration	-0.053	n.e.	n.e.	n.e.
	(4.11)			
Ageimig^2/100	0.028	n.e.	n.e.	n.e.
	(1.19)			
Mother foreign-born	n.e.	n.e.	n.e.	0.400
				(5.91)
Father foreign-born	n.e.	n.e.	n.e.	0.342
				(5.64)
Both parents foreign-born	n.e.	n.e.	n.e.	0.212
				(3.47)
Adjusted R^2	0.215	0.095	0.062	0.065
Sample size	7,496	4,506	56,483	60,989

Source: Current Population Survey, United States Census Bureau.

Note: Variables are as defined in Table 29 in Appendix.
  n.e. = Variable not entered.
  t statistics are in parentheses.

DISCUSSION

The results from the two different datasets generate very similar results. For the pooled sample and the foreign-born sample, educational attainment increases with age but at a decreasing rate. Being black or being Hispanic is associated with a lower educational attainment. Gender differentials persist among the foreign-born and the native-born, with men acquiring more education than women. As hypothesized, linguistic distance has a positive impact on educational attainment. Compared to native-born adults, immigrants from Africa, South and East Asia, and the Philippines acquire more education, while those from Mexico and Southern Europe acquire fewer years of education. Immigration after age 12 is associated with a lower educational level relative to natives, with those immigrating in the 13 to 19 age group exhibiting a particularly large negative differential with their native counterparts. This variation in educational attainment by age-at-immigration and country-of-origin also stands out in Gonzalez's (2001) study. He found that immigrants of Mexican and European descent who immigrate at younger ages (below age 9 and age 12, respectively) complete more years of schooling. For these immigrants, delayed entry results in lower overall education, and a lower percentage of U.S.-specific education. Our findings on the impact of immigrating at different age groups confirm Schaafsma and Sweetman's (1999) study, indicating a permanent negative effect on labor market outcomes of those immigrating in their teenage years.

The analysis on the foreign-born sample reflects some of the same trends observed in the pooled sample, especially with respect to country-of-origin and age-at-immigration. Our findings support our hypothesis that immigrants from non-English-speaking countries acquire more education than those from English-speaking countries.

The analysis of educational attainment by immigrant generation reveals that second-generation immigrants clearly have higher education levels compared to both first-generation and native-parentage adults. Whether or not first-generation immigrants acquire more or less schooling than their native counterparts depends on age-at-immigration. Our analysis suggests that first-generation immigrants arriving prior to age 13 acquire more schooling, or same years of schooling as their native counterparts. Our results on immigrant generation are similar to Rong and Grant's (1992) study. Based on a sample of 14 to 25-year-olds, Rong and Grant found that second-generation immigrants perform better academically than either first-generation or native-parentage adults, but first-generation youth who immigrate at very young ages exhibit schooling similar to that attained by second-generation and native-parentage youth.

CHAPTER 6

Preschool Enrollment of Immigrant Children

An important policy interest exists in the skill formation of immigrant children, and when they become adults, their labor market success. Initial conditions matter for subsequent success in school and in the workforce, as is emphasized in the path dependence literature. These initial conditions include whether children have access to opportunities during their preschool years to prepare them socially, psychologically, and intellectually for formal primary schooling. Perhaps more so than for the children of parents born and raised in the United States, preschool in the U.S. in a formal institutional setting may be crucial for the adjustment to primary schooling of immigrant children. This chapter examines preschool human capital accumulation, which is considered an important component of a child's educational attainment, by studying preschool enrollment among immigrant children and the U.S.-born children of immigrants.

EMPIRICAL ANALYSIS OF THE 1990 CENSUS DATA

The empirical analysis begins with the probit analyses of the pooled sample of first- and second-generation immigrant children along with native-parentage children. Then, a probit analysis on the first generation sample offers a comparison of school enrollment of first-generation immigrant children from different countries-of-origin. Lastly, the probits are run separately by immigrant generation to allow a comparative study of the relative importance of different determinants of school enrollment for each of the three groups.

School Enrollment of First-Generation, Second-Generation, and Native-Parentage Children

This section focuses on the pooled sample of 80,714 first-generation, second-generation, and native-parentage 3- to 5-year-old children. Comparative statistics for the three immigrant generations are summarized in Table 13. School enrollment is slightly lower for first-generation children (42%) compared to either the second-generation or native-parentage children (both at 43%). A much higher percentage of the first-generation and second-generation children are Hispanic when compared to the native-parentage children (over 40% versus 5%), but distribution of the three groups by black/non-black is about the same (6%). As can be expected, all native-parentage children are proficient in English, while about 95% of second-generation children are proficient, and about 83% of first-generation children are proficient. The average education level of the mother and the father rises with each immigrant generation – it is lowest for first-generation (11 years), increases by a year for second-generation, and by more than another year for the native-born parents.

The percentage of mothers with children below 5 years that participate in the labor market (either full-time or part-time) also rises substantially from first-generation (31%), to second-generation (47%), to native-parentage (55%) children. Perhaps the mother in a first-generation immigrant family is a tied mover and hence is more likely to have a lower labor force participation, particularly in the initial years after migration.

Probit results for the pooled sample are reported in Table 14A with predicted probabilities reported in Table 14B. Corresponding marginal effects are reported in Table 34, Appendix. The dependent variable for the probit equation was 'school enrollment,' the dichotomous variable for enrollment status (whether currently enrolled in school or not). Two different specifications were considered. The primary explanatory variables used in both specifications were male, black, Hispanic, South, rural, English proficiency, mother and father's education level, mother's labor force participation, household income, dichotomous variables representing number of siblings, and the child's age. The basic specification (column 1 in table 14A) was a simple model, which

TABLE 13. SUMMARY STATISTICS OF VARIABLES, FIRST-GENERATION, SECOND-GENERATION, AND NATIVE-PARENTAGE CHILDREN, UNITED STATES, 1990

AGE GROUP 3 TO 5 YEARS

Variable	First-Generation	Second-Generation	Native-Parentage
School enrollment	0.42 (0.49)	0.43 (0.49)	0.43 (0.50)
Male	0.51 (0.50)	0.51 (0.50)	0.51 (0.50)
Age	4.08 (0.83)	3.99 (0.82)	4.01 (0.82)
Age-at-immigration	1.82 (0.93)	n.a.	n.a.
Black	0.05 (0.21)	0.07 (0.25)	0.07 (0.26)
Hispanic	0.50 (0.50)	0.43 (0.49)	0.05 (0.21)
South	0.23 (0.42)	0.26 (0.44)	0.34 (0.47)
Rural	0.05 (0.21)	0.08 (0.28)	0.31 (0.46)
English proficiency	0.83 (0.38)	0.95 (0.21)	100.00 (0.04)
Mother's education	10.49 (4.83)	11.73 (3.98)	13.46 (2.14)
Father's education	11.19 (5.17)	12.11 (4.35)	13.66 (2.40)
Mother works full-time	0.23 (0.42)	0.34 (0.47)	0.33 (0.47)
Mother works part-time	0.08 (0.27)	0.13 (0.34)	0.22 (0.41)
Mother not working	0.69 (0.46)	0.53 (0.50)	0.45 (0.50)
Number of siblings	1.75 (1.50)	1.58 (1.22)	1.38 (1.01)
Only child	0.18 (0.38)	0.14 (0.35)	0.15 (0.36)
Household income	30800.16 (32964.88)	42429.30 (37026.46)	44130.63 (33453.64)
Sample size	1,556	9,392	69,766

Source: 1990 Census of Population of United States, Public Use Microdata Sample, 1% file.

Note: Variables are as defined in Table 29 in Appendix.
n.a. = Variable not applicable.
standard errors for all variables are in parentheses.

TABLE 14A. PROBIT ESTIMATES OF POOLED SAMPLE OF FIRST-GENERATION, SECOND-GENERATION, AND NATIVE-PARENTAGE CHILDREN, UNITED STATES, 1990

DEPENDENT VARIABLE: SCHOOL ENROLLMENT

AGE GROUP 3 TO 5 YEARS

Variable	(1)	(2)[a]
Constant	-1.426	-1.429
	(24.68)	(24.48)
Male	0.002	0.001
	(0.15)	(0.14)
Age3	-0.635	-0.635
	(52.11)	(52.13)
Age5	0.777	0.778
	(67.88)	(67.88)
Black	0.176	0.178
	(8.61)	(8.70)
Hispanic	0.003	0.007
	(0.14)	(0.35)
South	0.015	0.014
	(1.38)	(1.34)
Rural	-0.215	0.214
	(20.13)	(20.09)
English proficiency	-0.148	-0.153
	(3.10)	(3.18)
Mother's education	0.049	0.050
	(19.00)	(19.11)
Father's education	0.029	0.029
	(12.35)	(12.42)
Mother works full-time	0.036	0.036
	(3.16)	(3.14)
Mother works part-time	0.156	0.155
	(12.10)	(12.08)
1 Sibling	0.046	0.046
	(3.20)	(3.19)
2 Siblings	0.029	0.029
	(1.82)	(1.79)
3 Siblings	-0.055	0.056
	(2.62)	(2.64)
4+ Siblings	-0.082	-0.083
	(3.00)	(3.03)
Household income	5.46e-06	5.44e-06
	(32.33)	(32.14)
First-generation	0.243	n.e.
	(4.90)	
Second-generation	0.097	0.096
	(5.70)	(5.63)

TABLE 14A (continued)

Variable	(1)	(2)[a]
Age-at-immigration 2+	-0.163	-0.139
	(2.32)	(1.93)
BIRTHPLACE		
English-speaking countries	n.e.	0.483
		(3.27)
Africa	n.e.	0.088
		(0.34)
Mexico	n.e.	0.213
		(1.03)
Cuba	n.e.	0.197
		(1.53)
S. & C. America	n.e.	0.159
		(1.35)
Caribbean	n.e.	-0.343
		(1.38)
Southern Europe	n.e.	0.348
		(1.48)
E. & C. Europe	n.e.	-0.059
		(0.39)
N. & W. Europe	n.e.	1.196
		(3.24)
Philippines	n.e.	0.147
		(0.69)
China	n.e.	0.614
		(1.61)
Vietnam	n.e.	0.443
		(1.76)
East Asia	n.e.	0.257
		(2.02)
South Asia	n.e.	0.053
		(0.32)
Middle East	n.e.	-0.122
		(0.67)
Other Asia	n.e.	0.450
		(3.36)
Remaining countries	n.e.	0.554
		(3.31)
Pseudo R^2	0.174	0.174
Sample size	80,714	80,714

Source: 1990 Census of Population of United States, Public Use Microdata Sample, 1% file.

Note: Variables are as defined in Table 29 in Appendix.
n.e. = Variable not entered.   t statistics are in parentheses.
[a] benchmark group is all the 3- to 5-year age group native-parentage children.

TABLE 14B. PREDICTED PROBABILITIES OF SCHOOL ENROLLMENT FOR POOLED SAMPLE, UNITED STATES, 1990

AGE GROUP 3 TO 5 YEARS

Reference child[a]	0.38	Reference child[b]	0.38
Female	0.38	English-speaking countries	0.57*
Age3	0.17*	Africa	0.41
Age5	0.68*	Mexico	0.46
Black	0.45*	Cuba	0.81
Hispanic	0.38	S. & C. America	0.44
South	0.39	Caribbean	0.26
Rural	0.30*	Southern Europe	0.52
Not English-proficient	0.44*	E. & C. Europe	0.36
First-generation	0.48*	N. & W. Europe	0.81*
Second-generation	0.42*	Philippines	0.43
Age-at-immigration 2+	0.32*	China	0.62
1 Sibling	0.40*	Vietnam	0.55
2 Siblings	0.39	East Asia	0.48*
3 Siblings	0.36*	South Asia	0.40
4+ Siblings	0.35*	Middle East	0.33
Mother works full-time	0.40*	Other Asia	0.56*
Mother works part-time	0.44*		
Mother's education (mean=13.15)			
8	0.29*		
10	0.32*		
16	0.43*		
18	0.47*		

TABLE 14B (continued)

Reference child[a]	0.38
Father's education (mean=13.35)	
8	0.32*
10	0.34*
16	0.41*
18	0.43*
Household income (mean = 42937.7)	
20,000	0.33*
30,000	0.35*
60,000	0.42*
70,000	0.44*

Source: Table 14A

Reference child is a 4-year-old native white male with a non-working mother and no siblings, residing in an urban, non-south region with mean values for the continuous variables.

Note: [a] based on column (1) of Table 14A.
  [b] based on column (2) of Table 14A.
  * implies that estimated coefficients of the probit model were significant.

used the above-mentioned set of demographic and geographic variables as the explanatory variables. Additionally, it included two variables to explain the effects of first-generation and second-generation and a dichotomous variable on age-at-immigration to capture the effect, if any, of migrating prior to, versus migrating after, age 2 years. The second specification (column 2 in table 14A) added birthplace dichotomous variables to the original set of explanatory variables.

The reference child for the predicted probabilities in Table 14B for the pooled sample is defined as a 4-year-old native white male proficient in English with a non-working mother, no siblings, and residing in an urban, non-south region with mean variables for the continuous variables. The significant positive coefficients of both the immigrant generation variables indicate that first- and second-generation immigrants have a higher probability of being enrolled in preschool compared to a native parentage child. The predicted probability of preschool enrollment (column 1 of Table 14B) increases from 38 percent for native-parentage children to 48 percent for first-generation children, and to 42 percent for second-generation children. The negative coefficient of the age3 variable and the positive coefficient of the age5 variable indicates that the probability of enrollment in preschool increases with age. Blacks are more likely than non-blacks to be enrolled in preschool with the probability of enrollment increasing from 38 percent to 45 percent if a child is black rather than non-black. However, the Hispanic origin variable and the gender variable (male) are not significant. Living in rural areas has a strong negative effect on enrollment but the regional variable South is statistically insignificant.

The mother's labor supply variables have a positive and significant impact on school enrollment – the probability of enrollment increases from 38 percent to 40 percent if the mother works full-time, and to 44 percent if the mother works part-time. This finding is a little surprising given that mothers working full-time are more likely than those working part-time to use center-based care (Lehrer, 1983, 1989; Connelly and Kimmel, 2003). However, since more educated mothers are better aware of the benefits of preschool (Lehrer, 1989; Leibowitz et al., 1988), it is also likely that part-time working mothers as well as non-working mothers enroll their children in preschool for a few days a week.

The dichotomous variables for number of siblings indicate that children with one sibling are more likely to be enrolled in preschool than are children with no siblings. But children with three or more siblings are less likely to be enrolled than an only child. The impact of family size on preschool enrollment is thus non-linear. Given that preschools tend to be expensive and do not offer discounts for additional siblings, it is logical that preschool enrollment decreases as family size expands beyond a certain point.

As hypothesized, the education levels of the mother and the father have a positive and significant effect (Table 14A). The variable for the mother's education is more significant and has a higher magnitude than that of the father's education. The stronger impact of the mother's education is clear when we look at predicted probabilities (Table 14B): a decrease in the mother's education below the mean to 8 years reduces a child's probability of enrollment from 38 percent to 29 percent, but the same decrease in the father's education reduces the enrollment probability to 32 percent. Similarly, an increase in the level of the mother's education above the mean to 18 years increases the probability of enrollment to 47 percent, but the same increase in the father's education raises the enrollment probability to 43 percent. This finding is consistent with the strong positive relation between the mother's schooling and preschool enrollment, as established in the child care literature (Lehrer, 1989; Leibowitz et al., 1988).

Lastly, total family income has a strong positive effect on enrollment choice. To examine the effect of family income, we calculated probabilities at income levels below and above the mean. An increase in income from $20,000 to $70,000, for example, increases the probability of enrollment from 33 percent to 44 percent. Preschool is not mandatory, and unlike kindergarten, which is offered in public schools, preschool tends to be private and charges tuition. Therefore, holding other factors constant, preschool enrollment tends to increase with the level of the family's income.

The second specification (column 2 of table 14A) included the usual explanatory variables plus the birthplace dichotomous variables representing the children's country-of-origin. The benchmark was native-parentage children age 3 to 5 years; hence the coefficients represent the difference in enrollment between first-generation immigrant children from a particular country and all native-parentage children. Inclusion of the country-of-origin variables has a limited impact on the magnitudes or statistical significance of most of the variables in the original estimating equation. Most of the birthplace coefficients are statistically insignificant.[18] The only foreign country groups whose children are significantly different from native-parentage children are the English-speaking countries, North and West Europe, East Asia, Other Asia, and Mexico, and all five of them affect school enrollment positively. For example, the probability of school enrollment (Table 14B, column 2) increases from 38 percent for native-parentage, to 57 percent for immigrant children from English-speaking countries, and to 81 percent for immigrant children from North and West Europe, other variables being the same.

School Enrollment of First-Generation Children

This section discusses the sample of 1,556 first-generation 3- to 5-year-old children. Table 15 depicts the means and standard deviations of school enrollment by country-of-origin. As column 2 of Table 15 indicates, approximately 7% of immigrants are from English-speaking

TABLE 15. SUMMARY STATISTICS BY COUNTRY-OF-ORIGIN, FIRST-GENERATION, SECOND-GENERATION, AND NATIVE-PARENTAGE CHILDREN, UNITED STATES, 1990

AGE GROUP 3 TO 5 YEARS

Country-of-Origin	Sample Size	Percent of all Foreign-Born	Enrollment
English-speaking countries	91	0.06	0.61 (0.49)[a]
Africa	29	0.02	0.53 (0.50)
Mexico	588	0.38	0.34 (0.47)
Cuba	3	0.002	0.84 (0.37)
S. & C. America	148	0.10	0.44 (0.50)
Caribbean	38	0.02	0.23 (0.42)
Southern Europe	34	0.02	0.49 (0.50)
E. & C. Europe	89	0.06	0.48 (0.50)
N. & W. Europe	20	0.01	0.82 (0.38)
Philippines	41	0.03	0.50 (0.50)
China	13	0.01	0.58 (0.49)
Vietnam	28	0.02	0.46 (0.50)
East Asia	123	0.08	0.53 (0.50)
South Asia	73	0.05	0.47 (0.50)
Middle East	57	0.04	0.34 (0.48)
Other Asia	111	0.07	0.36 (0.48)
Remaining countries	70	0.05	0.50 (0.50)
Total	1,556	100	0.42 (0.49)

Source: 1990 Census of Population of United States, Public Use Microdata Sample, 1% file.

Note: Variables are as defined in Table 29 in Appendix.
[a] standard errors for all variables are indicated in parentheses.

countries (United Kingdom, England, Australia, New Zealand, British West Indies). The dominant immigrant source country is Mexico (above 30%), followed by South and Central America (10%), and East Asia (8%). Column 3 of the same table depicts that preschool enrollment is highest for immigrant children from Cuba and North and West Europe (82%), followed by English-speaking countries (61%), China (58%), and Africa and East Asia (53%). Immigrant children from the Caribbean (23%), Mexico, and the Middle East (34%), on the other hand, have the lowest enrollment rates.

Probit results for the first-generation sample are summarized in Table 16, Parts A and B. As in the analysis of the pooled sample, two different specifications were considered. The discussion here focuses on the probit coefficients and the predicted probabilities. Corresponding marginal effects are reported in Table 35, Appendix. Model (1) of the probit for the first-generation 3 to 5 age group sample (column 1 of table 16A) shows that mother's education, father's education, family income, and Hispanic are the only continuous variables statistically significant in explaining the probability of preschool enrollment among the foreign-born. While parental education and family income have a positive effect on school enrollment, being Hispanic has a negative effect.

When analyzing the first-generation sample, the reference child is a 4-year-old male immigrant from an English-speaking country with age-at-immigration less than 2 years. Preschool enrollment clearly increases with age since the probability of enrollment (column 1 of table 16B) increases from 15 to 34 to 69 percent from 3-year, to 4-year, to 5-year-olds, respectively. The positive coefficient on the two sibling dummy variables that are significant indicate that children with one sibling, as well as those with more than four siblings, have a higher probability of being enrolled in preschool compared to only children. Unlike in the pooled sample, the negative effect of increased family size on preschool enrollment is not that obvious among the first-generation immigrants.

The second specification (column 2 of table 16A) included the usual explanatory variables plus the birthplace variables. The benchmark was first-generation children from English-speaking countries in the 3 to 5 age group, hence the coefficients represent the difference in enrollment between first-generation children from a particular country and first-generation children from English-speaking countries. Inclusion of the country-of-origin dummy variables has no impact on the magnitudes or statistical significance of most of the

TABLE 16A. PROBIT ESTIMATES OF FIRST-GENERATION CHILDREN, UNITED STATES, 1990

DEPENDENT VARIABLE: SCHOOL ENROLLMENT

AGE GROUP 3 TO 5 YEARS

Variable	(1)	(2)[a]
Constant	-1.204	-0.865
	(5.89)	(3.21)
Male	0.060	0.052
	(0.86)	(0.73)
Age3	-0.645	-0.692
	(5.95)	(6.27)
Age5	0.891	0.902
	(9.15)	(9.14)
Black	-0.015	0.026
	(0.08)	(0.12)
Hispanic	-0.166	0.056
	(2.09)	(0.32)
South	0.094	0.051
	(1.13)	(0.59)
Rural	0.009	-0.002
	(0.06)	(0.01)
English proficiency	0.071	0.069
	(0.64)	(0.61)
Mother's education	0.026	0.025
	(2.40)	(2.22)
Father's education	0.023	0.023
	(2.29)	(2.21)
Mother works full-time	0.028	0.024
	(0.32)	(0.28)
Mother works part-time	0.205	0.180
	(1.52)	(1.31)
1 Sibling	0.274	0.313
	(2.63)	(2.94)
2 Siblings	0.093	0.101
	(0.81)	(0.86)
3 Siblings	0.089	0.147
	(0.63)	(1.01)
4+ Siblings	0.338	0.420
	(2.49)	(3.02)
Household income	4.49e-06	3.61e-06
	(4.08)	(3.31)
Age-at-immigration 2+	-0.165	-0.176
	(1.94)	(2.04)

TABLE 16A (continued)

Variable	(1)	(2)[a]
BIRTHPLACE		
Africa	n.e.	-0.315 (1.03)
Mexico	n.e.	-0.595 (2.55)
Cuba	n.e.	0.789 (0.94)
S. & C. America	n.e.	-0.427 (1.84)
Caribbean	n.e.	-0.847 (2.59)
Southern Europe	n.e.	-0.235 (0.82)
E. & C. Europe	n.e.	-0.542 (2.56)
N. & W. Europe	n.e.	0.762 (1.91)
Philippines	n.e.	-0.387 (1.45)
China	n.e.	0.185 (0.44)
Vietnam	n.e.	-0.330 (1.11)
East Asia	n.e.	-0.138 (0.70)
South Asia	n.e.	-0.469 (2.09)
Middle East	n.e.	-0.683 (2.90)
Other Asia	n.e.	-0.335 (1.58)
Remaining countries	n.e.	-0.093 (0.39)
Pseudo R^2	0.182	0.200
Sample size	1,556	1,556

Source: 1990 Census of Population of United States, Public Use Microdata Sample, 1% file.

Note: Variables are as defined in Table 29 in Appendix.
    n.e. = Variable not entered. t statistics are in parentheses.
    [a] benchmark group is all first-generation 3 to 5 year age group children from English-speaking countries.

**TABLE 16B. PREDICTED PROBABILITIES OF SCHOOL ENROLLMENT
FOR FIRST-GENERATION CHILDREN, UNITED STATES, 1990**

AGE GROUP 3 TO 5 YEARS

Reference child[a]	0.34	Reference child[b]	0.46
Female	0.32	Africa	0.34
Age3	0.15*	Mexico	0.24*
Age5	0.69*	Cuba	0.75
Black	0.34	S. & C. America	0.30
Hispanic	0.29*	Caribbean	0.17*
South	0.38	Southern Europe	0.37
Rural	0.35	E. & C. Europe	0.26*
Not English proficient	0.32	N. & W. Europe	0.74
Age-at-immigration 2+	0.29	Philippines	0.31
1 Sibling	0.45*	China	0.53
2 Siblings	0.38	Vietnam	0.33
3 Siblings	0.38	East Asia	0.40
4+ Siblings	0.47*	South Asia	0.28*
Mother works full-time	0.35	Middle East	0.21*
Mother works part-time	0.42	Other Asia	0.33
Mother's education (mean=10.37)			
8	0.32*		
12	0.36*		
16	0.40*		
18	0.42*		

TABLE 16B (continued)

Reference child	0.34
Father's education (mean=11.12)	
8	0.32*
12	0.35*
16	0.41*
18	0.41*
Household income (mean = 31,879)	
10,000	0.31*
20,000	0.32*
50,000	0.37*
60,000	0.39*

Source: Table 16A

Reference child is a 4-year-old male (non-black, non-Hispanic) immigrant (age-at-immigration less than 2) from an English-speaking country with a non-working mother and no siblings, residing in an urban, non-south region with mean values for the continuous variables.

Note: [a] based on column (1) of Table 16A.
[b] based on column (2) of Table 16A.
* implies that estimated coefficients of the probit model were significant.

variables in the original estimating equation. The only variable that is affected is Hispanic, which turns from negative significant to positive insignificant.[19] Moreover, only a few of the country-group variables show statistical significance. The only coefficients that are significant are Mexico, the Caribbean, East and Central Europe, South Asia, and the Middle East.[20] Thus, with these exceptions, other variables being the same, country-of-origin does not matter for preschool enrollment. Given the very different characteristics of immigrants from these five countries, holding other things constant, their foreign backgrounds (and thus their preference to rely on relative care when children are very

TABLE 17A. PROBIT ESTIMATES OF SECOND-GENERATION AND NATIVE-PARENTAGE CHILDREN, UNITED STATES, 1990

DEPENDENT VARIABLE: SCHOOL ENROLLMENT

AGE GROUP <u>3 TO 5</u> YEARS

Variable	Second-Generation	Native-Parentage	All Native-Born
Constant	-1.007	-1.699	-1.443
	(9.85)	(14.17)	(21.92)
Male	0.006	-0.001	0.001
	(0.20)	(0.04)	(0.02)
Age3	-0.683	-0.631	-0.635
	(19.14)	(48.21)	(51.79)
Age5	0.863	0.772	0.777
	(24.37)	(63.08)	(67.33)
Black	0.198	0.194	0.181
	(3.19)	(8.87)	(8.78)
Hispanic	-0.110	-0.014	-0.007
	(3.20)	(0.55)	(0.34)
South	0.090	0.006	0.014
	(2.73)	(0.56)	(1.34)
Rural	-0.154	-0.205	-0.212
	(3.31)	(18.56)	(19.84)
English proficiency	-0.025	-0.139	-0.172
	(0.37)	(1.22)	(3.05)
Mother's education	0.029	0.062	0.052
	(5.62)	(19.67)	(19.30)
Father's education	0.012	0.038	0.030
	(2.45)	(13.38)	(12.35)
Mother works full-time	0.015	0.039	0.034
	(0.45)	(3.19)	(3.00)
Mother works part-time	0.118	0.154	0.155
	(2.69)	(11.31)	(11.94)
1 Sibling	0.056	0.035	0.040
	(1.26)	(2.23)	(2.75)
2 Siblings	0.114	0.009	0.026
	(2.38)	(0.54)	(1.59)
3 Siblings	0.017	-0.078	-0.060
	(0.29)	(3.40)	(2.79)
4+ Siblings	0.033	-0.156	-0.108
	(0.47)	(5.05)	(3.85)

TABLE 17A (continued)

Variable	Second-Generation	Native-Parentage	All Native-Born
Household income	5.09e-06 (11.22)	5.22e-06 (28.04)	5.41e-06 (31.57)
Mother foreign-born	n.e.	n.e.	0.051 (1.57)
Father foreign-born	n.e.	n.e.	0.076 (2.52)
Both parents foreign-born	n.e	n.e	0.130 (5.78)
Pseudo R^2	0.197	0.173	0.174
Sample size	9,392	69,766	79,158

Source: 1990 Census of Population of United States, Public Use Microdata Sample, 1% file.

Note: Variables are as defined in Table 29 in appendix.
    n.e. = Variable not entered.
    t statistics are in parentheses.

young) probably account for their low preschool enrollment. For example, the probability of school enrollment (column 1 of table 16B) decreases from 46 percent for immigrant children from English-speaking countries, to 28 percent for immigrant children from South Asia, and to 17 percent for Caribbean immigrant children. This may reflect a preference for care provided by relatives among immigrants from these countries.

Comparative Study of First-Generation, Second-Generation, and Native-Parentage Children

Probit equations estimated separately for first-generation, second-generation, and native-parentage children are presented in Table 17, A and B. Corresponding marginal effects are reported in Appendix, Table 36. The coefficients of the native-parentage sample probit are very similar to the pooled sample probit coefficients because natives-borns constitute approximately 86% of the total pooled sample in each age group.

TABLE 17B. PREDICTED PROBABILITIES OF SECOND-GENERATION AND NATIVE-PARENTAGE CHILDREN, UNITED STATES, 1990

AGE GROUP 3 TO 5 YEARS

Variable	Second-Generation	Native-Parentage	All Native-Born
Reference child	0.37[a]	0.39[b]	0.38[c]
Female	0.37	0.39	0.38
Age3	0.16*	0.18*	0.18*
Age5	0.70*	0.69*	0.68*
Black	0.45*	0.47*	0.45*
Hispanic	0.33*	0.39	0.39
South	0.41*	0.39	0.39
Rural	0.31*	0.32*	0.31*
Not English proficient	0.38	0.45	0.45*
1 Sibling	0.39	0.41*	0.40*
2 Siblings	0.41*	0.40	0.39
3 Siblings	0.38	0.36*	0.36*
4+ Siblings	0.38	0.33*	0.34*
Mother works full-time	0.38	0.41*	0.40*
Mother works part-time	0.42*	0.45*	0.44*
Mother foreign-born	n.e.	n.e.	0.46
Father foreign-born	n.e.	n.e.	0.47*
Both parents foreign-born	n.e.	n.e.	0.50*

TABLE 17B (continued)

Variable	Second-Generation	Native-Parentage	All Native-Born
Reference child	0.37[a]	0.39[b]	0.38[c]
Mother's education (mean=11.7d[d];13.4[e];13.2[f])			
8	0.33*	0.27*	0.29*
10	0.35*	0.32*	0.32*
16	0.42*	0.46*	0.44*
18	0.44*	0.50*	0.48*
Father's education (mean=12.04[d];13.58[e];13.40[f])			
8	0.35*	0.31*	0.32*
10	0.36*	0.34*	0.34*
16	0.39*	0.43*	0.42*
18	0.40*	0.46*	0.44*
HH income (mean=42676[d];43220[e];43155[f])			
10,000	0.31*	0.33*	0.32*
20,000	0.30*	0.35*	0.34*
50,000	0.38*	0.41*	0.40*
60,000	0.40*	0.43*	0.42*

Source: Table 17A

Reference child is a 4-year-old native white male with a non-working mother and no siblings, residing in an urban, non-south region with mean values for the continuous variables.

Note: [a] based on column (1) of Table 17A.
  [b] based on column (2) of Table 17A.
  [c] based on column (3) of Table 17A.
  [d] means for second-generation, [e] means for native, [f] means for all native-born.
  * implies that estimated coefficients of the probit model were significant

Major differences are observed across the three immigrant generations regarding the effect of race/ethnicity and parental education. The race variable, black, is not significant in explaining the preschool enrollment for first-generation children. However, for both second-generation and native-parentage children, being black has a positive impact on probability of preschool enrollment, other variables being the same. This result contradicts Brayfield and Hofferth's (1995) finding that black mothers are less likely to use paid care for their preschoolers, possibly because this study is of two-parent households. Being Hispanic, on the other hand, does not impact the enrollment probability for native-parentage children, but it reduces the probability of preschool enrollment for second-generation as well as first-generation children.

The effect of the mother and father's education level is less pronounced in the first- and second-generation compared to the native-parentage generation. Perhaps for second-generation and first-generation immigrants, parental education is not a good measure of parental influence. As the mother's education increases from 8 years to 18 years, the probability of enrollment increases from 33 percent to 44 percent for first-generation and second-generation children. For the same increase in the mother's education, the enrollment probability increases from 27 percent to 50 percent for the native-parentage children.

To study the effect of foreign-parentage on preschool enrollment, the analysis focuses on the sample of all native-born adults (i.e., second-generation and native-parentage children). Three variables are introduced into the basic regression specification, mother-only foreign-born, father-only foreign-born, and both parents foreign-born. The results indicate that having a foreign-born father or having both parents foreign-born raises the probability of preschool enrollment compared to having both parents native-born (Table 17, A and B).

Parents do not appear to treat their 3- to 5-year-old sons differently than their daughters. The dichotomous gender variables have very small coefficients and are not statistically significant. When the equations are computed separately for boys and girls, the coefficients do not vary by gender.

EMPIRICAL ANALYSIS OF THE OCTOBER 1995 CPS DATA

This section repeats the analysis conducted in the previous section using the October 1995 CPS dataset. In analyzing the CPS dataset, we faced some data constraints because the econometric analysis of the

Census could not be exactly replicated. Firstly, there was no usable information to construct two variables important to our analysis, namely, number of siblings and English proficiency. Second, due to the much smaller size of the CPS dataset, it was econometrically difficult to conduct some of the detailed analysis by country-of-origin for each age group using the CPS data. Third, the CPS asked school enrollment questions to three distinct populations: 3 to 5 years, 6 to 14 years, and 15 years and older. Given the nature of the enrollment question, the age group classification adopted in analyzing the CPS data is slightly different from the age group classification used in the Census data (age group 3 to 5, 6 to 14, and 15 to 18; instead of age group 3 to 5, 6 to 15, and 16 to 18).

School Enrollment of First-Generation, Second-Generation, and Native-Parentage Children

This section discusses the results for the pooled sample of 4,327 first-generation, second-generation, and native-parentage 3- to 5-year-old children. Comparative statistics for first-generation, second-generation, and native-parentage children for the two age groups are summarized in Table 18. School enrollment is highest for the native-parentage children (67%) followed by first-generation children (65%), and second-generation children (55%). The percentage of Hispanics is much higher in the first- and second-generation (above 50%) compared to the native-parentage sample (5%). On the other hand, the native-parentage sample has a higher percentage of blacks compared to the first- and second- generation. The native-parentage families also tend to reside more often in the South and in non-metropolitan areas compared to the two immigrant generations. The average education level of the mother and the father is about the same in the first- and second-generation sample (12 years) but is higher (13.8 years) for native-parentage children. In line with our finding for the Census data, the percentage of working mothers rises from the first-generation (40%), to second-generation (48%), to native-parentage (63%).

The probit results for the pooled sample are summarized in Table 19, Parts A and B. The discussion here focuses on the probit coefficients and on the predicted probabilities. Corresponding marginal effects are reported in Table 37, Appendix. The dependent variable for the probit equation was 'school enrollment', but only one specification was considered. The primary explanatory variables used were male, black, Hispanic, South, rural, household income, mother and father's

TABLE 18. SUMMARY STATISTICS OF VARIABLES, FIRST-GENERATION, SECOND-GENERATION, AND NATIVE-PARENTAGE CHILDREN, UNITED STATES, 1995

AGE GROUP <u>3 TO 5</u> YEARS

Variable	First-Generation	Second-Generation	Native-Parentage
School enrollment	0.65	0.55	0.67
	(0.47)	(0.50)	(0.47)
Male	0.60	048	0.50
	(0.49)	(0.50)	(0.50)
Age	3.95	3.98	4.01
	(0.78)	(0.23)	(0.82)
Age-at-immigration	1.78	n.a.	n.a.
	(0.91)		
Black	0.03	0.05	0.09
	(0.17)	(0.23)	(0.29)
Hispanic	0.51	0.56	0.05
	(0.50)	(0.50)	(0.22)
South	0.31	0.23	0.36
	(0.46)	(0.42)	(0.48)
Non-MSA	0.07	0.07	0.23
	(0.25)	(0.25)	(0.42)
Mother's education	11.72)	11.77	13.75
	(4.26)	(3.68)	(2.48)
Father's education	11.92	11.42	13.83
	(4.86)	(4.24)	(2.31)
Mother works full-time	0.32	0.34	0.37
	(0.47)	(0.47)	(0.48)
Mother works part-time	0.08	0.14	0.25
	(0.27)	(0.35)	(0.43)
Mother not working	0.60	0.52	0.37
	(0.49)	(0.50)	(0.48)
Household income	27349	29709	42994
	(27701)	(25013)	(26223)
Sample size	78	708	3,541

Source: October 1995 Current Population Survey, United States Census Bureau.

Note: Variables are as defined in Table 29 in appendix.
       n.a. = Variable not applicable.
       standard errors for all variables are in parentheses.

TABLE 19A. PROBIT ESTIMATES OF POOLED SAMPLE OF FIRST-GENERATION, SECOND-GENERATION, AND NATIVE-PARENTAGE CHILDREN, UNITED STATES, 1995

DEPENDENT VARIABLE: SCHOOL ENROLLMENT

AGE GROUP 3 TO 5 YEARS

Variable	(1)
Constant	-1.050
	(6.74)
Male	-0.079
	(1.76)
Age3	-0.691
	(13.89)
Age5	1.36
	(20.79)
Black	0.020
	(0.22)
Hispanic	0.056
	(0.65)
South	0.015
	(0.29)
Non-MSA	-0.196
	(3.53)
First-generation	0.453
	(1.88)
Second-generation	-0.123
	(1.77)
Age-at-immigration 2+	-0.217
	(0.61)
Household income	7.25e-06
	(6.99)
Mother's education	0.052
	(4.13)
Father's education	0.031
	(2.73)
Mother works full-time	0.032
	(0.62)
Mother works part-time	0.206
	(3.43)
Pseudo R^2	0.262
Sample size	4,327

Source: October 1995 Current Population Survey, United States Census Bureau.

Note: Variables are as defined in Table 29 in Appendix.
    n.e. = Variable not entered.

TABLE 19B. PREDICTED PROBABILITIES OF SCHOOL ENROLLMENT FOR POOLED SAMPLE, UNITED STATES, 1995

AGE GROUP <u>3 TO 5</u> YEARS

Reference child[a]	0.61
Female	0.64
Age3	0.34*
Age5	0.95*
Black	0.62
Hispanic	0.63
South	0.62
Non-MSA	0.53*
First-generation	0.77
Second-generation	0.56
Age-at-immigration 2+	0.52
Mother works full-time	0.62
Mother works part-time	0.69*
Mother's education (mean=13.44)	
8	0.50*
10	0.54*
16	0.66*
18	0.70*

TABLE 19B (continued)

Reference child[a]	0.61
Father's education (mean=13.50)	
8	0.54*
10	0.57*
16	0.64*
18	0.66*
Household income (mean =40,375)	
10,000	0.52*
20,000	0.55*
60,000	0.66*
70,000	0.69*

Source: Table 19A

Reference child is a 4-year-old native white male with a non-working mother and no siblings, residing in a metropolitan, non-south region with mean values for the continuous variables.

Note: [a] based on column (1) of Table 19A.
* implies that estimated coefficients of the probit model were significant.

education level, mother's labor force participation, and dummy variables for age and age-at-immigration. This specification (column 1 in table 19A) simply used the above-mentioned set of demographic and geographic variables as the explanatory variables, plus variables first-generation, second-generation, and age-at-immigration to capture the effects of immigrant generation on school enrollment. The probit model shows that both immigrant generation variables as well as the age-at-immigration dummy are statistically insignificant. The negative sign on the age3 variable and the positive sign on the age5 variable indicate that preschool enrollment increases with age. Moreover, residing in a non-metropolitan area decreases the probability of preschool enrollment from 61% to 53% (Table 19B). Only one of the two mother's labor supply variables has a significant impact on school enrollment – the probability of enrollment increases from 61% for mother not-working to 69% if the mother works part-time. Both the parental education variables have a positive and significant effect. Similar to the Census findings, the mother's education is more significant and has a higher magnitude than that of the father's education. The stronger impact of the mother's education is obvious when we look at predicted probabilities: a similar increase or decrease in the mother's and father's education raises or lowers the probability of enrollment by different magnitudes (always larger magnitudes associated with the mother's education). Furthermore, the probability of enrollment increases from 0.61 (at the mean) to 0.66 at an income slightly above the mean, and falls to 0.55 at an income slightly below the mean, thus signifying the importance of family income in preschool enrollment.

Comparative Study of First-Generation, Second-Generation, and Native-Parentage Children

Probits estimated separately for the first-generation, second-generation and native-parentage children are presented in Table 20, Parts A and B. Corresponding marginal effects are reported in Table 38, Appendix. For both the age groups being discussed, the sample size of first-generation was extremely small (78 observations). Moreover, certain explanatory variables had to be dropped from the probit model because they predicted the outcome perfectly, and this problem in turn reduced the probit sample size even further making it statistically inappropriate to estimate the model. Therefore, for the 3 to 5 age group, we only examine differences in the enrollment probit between the second-generation children and native-parentage children. For native-parentage children, parental education, family income, and mother working part-time are statistically significant, but none of the explanatory variables are significant for the second-generation sample. Furthermore, to analyze the effect of foreign-parentage on preschool enrollment patterns of U.S.-born children, we introduced three variables: mother-only foreign-born, father-only foreign-born, and both parents foreign-born in a specification combining all second-generation and native-parentage children. However, all three foreign-parentage variables were statistically insignificant.

**TABLE 20A. PROBIT ESTIMATES OF SECOND-GENERATION AND
NATIVE-PARENTAGE CHILDREN, UNITED STATES, 1995**

DEPENDENT VARIABLE: SCHOOL ENROLLMENT

AGE GROUP 3 TO 5 YEARS

Variable	Second-Generation	Native-Parentage	All Native-Born
Constant	-0.454 (1.58)	-1.329 (6.67)	-1.053 (6.55)
Male	-0.181 (1.60)	-0.069 (1.39)	-0.081 (1.79)
Age3	-0.944 (7.42)	-0.643 (11.78)	-0.690 (13.81)
Age5	1.417 (9.03)	1.343 (18.50)	1.350 (20.56)
Black	0.295 (1.12)	-0.036 (0.36)	0.007 (0.07)
Hispanic	-0.218 (1.56)	0.132 (1.04)	0.029 (0.33)
South	-0.151 (1.01)	0.045 (0.80)	0.012 (0.24)
Non-MSA	-0.186 (0.88)	-0.174 (2.99)	-0.195 (3.49)
Household income	2.07e-06 (0.81)	7.77e-06 (6.66)	7.16e-06 (6.84)
Mother's education	0.020 (0.88)	0.071 (4.60)	0.052 (4.05)
Father's education	0.039 (1.81)	0.028 (1.99)	0.032 (2.75)
Mother works full-time	0.023 (0.18)	0.024 (0.41)	0.034 (0.64)
Mother works part-time	0.197 (1.18)	0.207 (3.18)	0.029 (0.33)
Mother foreign-born	n.e.	n.e.	0.012 (0.24)
Father foreign-born	n.e.	n.e.	-0.195 (3.49)
Both parents foreign-born	n.e.	n.e.	-0.099 (1.16)
Pseudo R^2	0.317	0.250	0.260
Sample size	708	3,541	4,249

Source: October 1995 Current Population Survey, United States Census Bureau.

Note: Variables are as defined in Table 29 in appendix.
     n.e. = Variable not entered. t statistics are in parentheses.

**TABLE 20B. PREDICTED PROBABILITIES OF SECOND-GENERATION
AND NATIVE-PARENTAGE CHILDREN, UNITED STATES, 1995**

AGE GROUP 3 TO 5 YEARS

Variable	Second-Generation	Native-Parentage	All Native-Born
Reference child	0.56[a]	0.62[b]	0.61[c]
Female	0.63	0.64	0.64
Age3	0.21*	0.36*	0.34*
Age5	0.94*	0.95*	0.95*
Black	0.67	0.60	0.61
Hispanic	0.47	0.67	0.62
South	0.50	0.63	0.62
Non-MSA	0.49	0.55*	0.54*
Mother works full-time	0.57	0.62	0.63
Mother works part-time	0.64	0.69*	0.69*
Mother foreign-born	n.e.	n.e.	0.62
Father foreign-born	n.e.	n.e.	0.65
Both parents foreign-born	n.e.	n.e.	0.65
Mother's education (mean=12.19[d];13.72[e];13.46[f])			
8	0.53	0.46*	0.50*
10	0.54	0.51*	0.54*
16	0.59	0.68*	0.66*
18	0.61	0.73*	0.70*

TABLE 20B (continued)

Variable	Second-Generation	Native-Parentage	All Native-Born
Reference child	0.56[a]	0.62[b]	0.61[c]
Father's education (mean=12.05[d];13.82[e];13.52[f])			
8	0.50	0.55*	0.54*
10	0.53	0.58*	0.57*
16	0.62	0.64*	0.64*
18	0.65	0.66*	0.67*
Household income (mean=32,424[d]; 42241[e];40605[f])			
10,000	0.54	0.52*	0.53*
20,000	0.55	0.55*	0.55*
60,000	0.58	0.67*	0.66*

Source: Table 20A

Reference child is a 4-year-old native white male with a non-working mother and no siblings, residing in a metropolitan, non-south region with mean values for the continuous variables.

Note: [a] based on column (1) of Table 20A;
[b] based on column (2) of Table 20A;
[c] based on column (3) of Table 20A.
[d] means for second-generation, [e] means for native-parentage, [f] means for all native-born.
* implies that estimated coefficients of the probit model were significant.

DISCUSSION

An increasing percentage of children today receive some form of preschool instruction. Social scientists have often indicated the short-term (achievement test gains) and long-term benefits (increased likelihood of completing high school[21]) associated with preschool education. However, preschool programs are typically private and charge tuition, thereby it is not surprising to find differences in enrollment rates by family income and race/ethnicity. Since preschool education is believed to be an important education resource, and yet its access is limited to children from economically better off families, the federal government initiated programs such as Head Start to allow children from low-income families to enroll in preschool. For the purpose of this analysis, preschool included all center-based programs such as Head Start, nursery school, day care, and kindergarten.

The Census results indicate a higher probability of preschool enrollment among first- and second-generation immigrant children as compared to native-parentage children. However, the CPS results indicate that both immigrant generation variables are statistically insignificant. Both datasets depict that the probability of being enrolled in preschool increases with age, but the age-at-immigration dummy variable is not very significant in explaining preschool enrollment. For the pooled sample, the mother's labor force participation and parental education have a strong positive effect on the probability of preschool enrollment. Importantly, the pooled sample analyses of both datasets indicate that the mother's education is more important than the father's education. That the mother's education has a stronger impact on child's attainment than the father's education was found earlier by Schultz (1984) and Manski et al. (1992). Furthermore, household income has a strong positive association with the probability of being enrolled in preschool. When looking at differences by country-of-origin, most coefficients are insignificant. But immigrants from North and West Europe, English-speaking countries, and East Asia exhibit a higher probability of enrollment relative to the native-parentage children. The Census also indicates that children with both parents foreign-born and those with father-only foreign-born have a higher probability of being enrolled than do children with both parents native-born.

CHAPTER 7

High School Enrollment of Youth Immigrants

The completion of high school is very important due to the increased employment opportunity and income potential associated with high school and college completion. The transition from school to work is particularly difficult for those who drop out of school and thus are not high school graduates. Moreover, teenagers who do not complete high school have substantially lower employment rates and lifetime earnings than the more educated. Yet our data (see chapter 4) indicates that a substantial percentage of teenagers drop out of high school. To understand the low school enrollment rates among teenagers, this chapter uses data from the 1990 Census of Population and Housing and the 1995 Current Population Survey to investigate the determinants of school enrollment among 15- to 18-year-olds.

EMPIRICAL ANALYSIS OF THE 1990 CENSUS DATA

A comparative analysis of school enrollment among the two immigrant generation groups and the native-parentage children is conducted using the pooled sample of first- and second-generation immigrant children and native-parentage children. A probit analysis on the first-generation sample enables a detailed comparison of the school enrollment among first-generation immigrant children with different characteristics (country-of-origin, age-at-immigration). Finally, probits run separately on the first-generation, second-generation, and native-parentage sample give a picture of the relative importance of different determinants of school enrollment for each of the three generations.

School Enrollment of First-Generation, Second-Generation, and Native-Parentage Children

This section discusses the pooled sample of 65,718 first-generation, second-generation, and native-parentage 16- to 18-year-old children. Comparative statistics for first-generation, second-generation, and native-parentage children for the two age groups are summarized in Table 21. For this late-teen group, school enrollment is slightly higher for the second-generation (91%) compared to the first-generation and native-parentage children (90%). The distribution of blacks/non-blacks and Hispanics/non-Hispanics is quite uniform among the two immigrant generations and the native-parentage children. As expected, most second-generation teenagers are proficient in English, but about 11% of first-generation teenagers report either poor or no English speaking skills. Similar to the 3 to 5 age group, the average level of education of both parents increases with each subsequent generation, as does the percentage of mothers working. Moreover, for the native-parentage, as well as for the two immigrant generations, the level of the mother's labor force participation is substantially higher in the 16 to 18 age group compared to the 3 to 5 age group: 55% for the first-generation, 59% for the second-generation, and 70% for the native-parentage.

Probit results for the pooled sample are summarized in Table 22, A and B. The discussion here focuses on the sign and statistical significance of the probit coefficients and on the predicted probabilities derived from the probit model. Corresponding marginal effects are reported in Table 39, Appendix. The dependent variable for the probit equation was 'school enrollment', the dichotomous variable for enrollment status (whether currently enrolled in school or not). Two different specifications were considered. As in the analysis for preschoolers, the primary explanatory variables used in both specifications were male, black, Hispanic, South, rural, English proficiency, mother and father's education level, mother's labor force participation, household income, dummy variables for age, and dummy variables representing number of siblings. The basic specification (column 1 in table 22A) was a simple model, which primarily used the demographic and geographic variables as the explanatory variables. Additionally, it included two variables to explain the effects of first-generation, second-generation, and dummy variables reflecting age-at-immigration groups. The second specification (column 2 in table 22A) added birthplace dummy variables as well. The benchmark age group in the probit equation is 16 years and the benchmark age-at-immigration group is those immigrating between 0 and 4 years.

TABLE 21. SUMMARY STATISTICS OF VARIABLES, FIRST-GENERATION, SECOND-GENERATION, AND NATIVE-PARENTAGE CHILDREN, UNITED STATES, 1990

AGE GROUP <u>16 TO 18</u> YEARS

Variable	First-Generation	Second-Generation	Native-Parentage
School enrollment	0.90 (0.31)	0.91 (0.28)	0.90 (0.31)
Male	0.53 (0.50)	0.54 (0.50)	0.52 (0.50)
Age	16.97 (0.81)	16.94 (0.81)	16.94 (0.80)
Age-at-immigration	8.23 (4.86)	n.a.	n.a.
Black	0.07 (0.25)	0.05 (0.21)	0.09 (0.29)
Hispanic	0.43 (0.49)	0.37 (0.48)	0.36 (0.48)
South	0.24 (0.43)	0.25 (0.43)	0.36 (0.48)
Rural	0.05 (0.22)	0.12 (0.33)	0.36 (0.48)
English proficiency	0.89 (0.31)	0.98 (0.14)	0.99 (0.08)
Mother's education	9.70 (4.72)	11.38 (3.96)	12.95 (2.21)
Father's education	10.59 (5.07)	11.73 (4.54)	13.22 (2.79)
Mother works full-time	0.44 (0.50)	0.42 (0.49)	0.49 (0.50)
Mother works part-time	0.11 (0.31)	0.17 (0.37)	0.21 (0.41)
Mother not working	0.45 (0.49)	0.41 (0.49)	0.30 (0.46)
Number of siblings	1.38 (1.50)	0.98 (1.21)	0.79 (1.05)
Only child	0.36 (0.48)	0.46 (0.50)	0.51 (0.50)
Net income	42317 (35023)	56488 (45551)	55196 (37666)
Sample size	3,560	5,401	56,757

Source: 1990 Census of Population of United States, Public Use Microdata Sample, 1% file.

Note: Variables are as defined in Table 29 in appendix.
     n.a. = Variable not applicable.
     standard errors for all variables are in parentheses.

TABLE 22A. PROBIT ESTIMATES OF POOLED SAMPLE OF FIRST-GENERATION, SECOND-GENERATION, AND NATIVE-PARENTAGE CHILDREN, UNITED STATES, 1990

DEPENDENT VARIABLE: SCHOOL ENROLLMENT

AGE GROUP <u>16 TO 18</u> YEARS

Variable	(1)	(2)[a]
Constant	-0.057	-0.091
	(0.82)	(1.28)
Male	-0.065	-0.066
	(4.61)	(4.64)
Age17	-0.210	-0.211
	(10.86)	(10.90)
Age18	-0.829	-0.830
	(44.23)	(44.22)
Black	0.056	0.058
	(2.05)	(2.14)
Hispanic	0.037	0.073
	(1.29)	(2.36)
South	-0.036	-0.035
	(2.39)	(2.33)
Rural	0.055	0.059
	(3.62)	(3.85)
English proficiency	0.367	0.382
	(6.69)	(6.89)
Mother's education	0.049	0.050
	(14.25)	(14.50)
Father's education	0.045	0.045
	(15.72)	(15.54)
Mother works full-time	0.038	0.038
	(2.30)	(2.30)
Mother works part-time	0.096	0.098
	(4.64)	(4.71)
1 Sibling	0.136	0.135
	(7.49)	(7.42)
2 Siblings	0.074	0.072
	(3.14)	(3.04)
3 Siblings	0.029	0.025
	(0.81)	(0.71)
4+ Siblings	-0.089	-0.090
	(2.17)	(2.18)
Net income	1.98e-06	2.01e-06
	(7.96)	(8.06)
First-generation	0.424	n.e.
	(6.73)	
Second-generation	0.302	0.291
	(10.02)	(9.52)

TABLE 22A (continued)

Variable	(1)	(2)[a]
Age-at-immigration 5 to 12	0.107 (1.41)	0.056 (0.71)
Age-at-immigration 13 to 18	-0.171 (2.01)	-0.214 (2.49)
BIRTHPLACE		
English-speaking countries	n.e.	0.328 (2.31)
Africa	n.e.	0.328 (1.01)
Mexico	n.e.	0.365 (1.90)
Cuba	n.e.	0.290 (1.46)
S. & C. America	n.e.	0.381 (3.26)
Caribbean	n.e.	1.181 (3.94)
Southern Europe	n.e.	0.397 (2.09)
E. & C. Europe	n.e.	0.302 (1.81)
N. & W. Europe	n.e.	-0.065 (0.18)
Philippines	n.e.	0.135 (0.92)
China	n.e.	0.769 (3.72)
Vietnam	n.e.	0.781 (5.48)
East Asia	n.e.	0.632 (3.95)
South Asia	n.e.	1.088 (3.04)
Middle East	n.e.	0.432 (2.28)
Other Asia	n.e.	0.932 (6.12)
Remaining countries	n.e.	0.146 (0.76)
Pseudo R^2	0.111	0.112
Sample size	65,718	65,718

Source: 1990 Census of Population of United States, Public Use Microdata Sample, 1% file.

Note: Variables are as defined in Table 29 in appendix.
   n.e. = Variable not entered. t statistics are in parentheses.
   [a] benchmark group is all 3 to 5 year age group native-parentage children.

TABLE 22B. PREDICTED PROBABILITIES OF SCHOOL ENROLLMENT FOR POOLED SAMPLE, UNITED STATES, 1990

AGE GROUP 16 TO 18 YEARS

Reference child[a]	0.76	Reference child[b]	0.76
Female	0.78*	English-speaking countries	0.85*
Age16	0.94*	Africa	0.85
Age17	0.91*	Mexico	0.86
Black	0.78*	Cuba	0.84
Hispanic	0.77	S. & C. America	0.86*
South	0.75*	Caribbean	0.97*
Rural	0.78*	Southern Europe	0.87*
Not English proficient	0.64*	E. & C. Europe	0.85
First-generation	0.87*	N. & W. Europe	0.74
Second-generation	0.85*	Philippines	0.80
Age-at-immigration 5 to 12	0.80	China	0.93*
Age-at-immigration 13 to 18	0.71*	Vietnam	0.93*
1 Sibling	0.80*	East Asia	0.91*
2 Siblings	0.79*	South Asia	.96*
3 Siblings	0.77	Middle East	0.87*
4+ Siblings	0.74*	Other Asia	0.95*
Mother works full-time	0.77*		
Mother works part-time	0.79*		

TABLE 22B (continued)

Reference child[a]	0.76
Mother's education (mean=12.60)	
8	0.69*
10	0.72*
16	0.81*
18	0.84*
Father's education (mean=12.87)	
8	0.69*
10	0.72*
16	0.81*
18	0.83*
Net income (mean = 51923.8)	
20,000	0.74*
30,000	0.75*
60,000	0.77*
70,000	0.77*

Source: Table 22A

Reference child is an 18-year-old native white male with a non-working mother and no siblings, residing in an urban, non-south region with mean values for the continuous variables.

Note: [a] based on column (1) of Table 22A.
     [b] based on column (2) of Table 22A.
     * implies that estimated coefficients of the probit model were significant.

Model (1) of the probit for the total 16 to 18 age group pooled sample depicts that most coefficients, except Hispanic, certain age-at-immigration dummy variables, and sibling dummy variables, are statistically significant. In contrast to the 3 to 5 age group, the gender variable (male) has a negative impact on school enrollment, and English proficiency has a positive impact on school enrollment. The reference group in the pooled sample predicted probability calculation (Table 22B) is an 18-year-old native white male with a non-working mother and no siblings, residing in an urban, non-south region with mean values for continuous variables. The negative coefficient of the gender variable 'male' reflects that male teenagers are less likely to be enrolled in school relative to their female counterparts. Male 18-year-olds have a slightly lower probability of being enrolled (0.76) compared to female teenagers of the same age (0.78). Besides, the probability of enrollment in high school drops from 0.76 for children with good English proficiency to 0.64 for those with poor English proficiency. The negative sign on the age dummy variables reflects that 17-year-olds and 18-year-olds have a lower probability of being enrolled in high school than 16-year-olds. In fact, the probability of school enrollment decreases progressively between age 16 and age 18.

The positive sign on the immigrant generation variables implies that both second-generation and first-generation children have a higher probability of being in high school relative to their native counterparts. The probability of enrollment increases from 0.76 for native-parentage children, to 0.85 for second-generation, and 0.87 for first-generation children. In terms of the impact on high school enrollment, immigrating between 5 and 12 years of age is no different than immigrating between 0 and 4 years. However, immigrating as a teenager does have a negative impact on enrollment in high school. The two demographic variables, South and rural, as well as the race variable, black, are small in magnitude and in statistical significance. The mother's labor supply variables have a positive and significant impact on school enrollment. As a child grows older, the positive effect of the mother's labor force participation (contribution to family income) dominates the negative impact of her absence. The predicted probabilities on the number of siblings reflect that teenagers with no siblings are less likely to be enrolled in high school compared to teenagers with one or two siblings. However, the probability of enrollment does fall as family size increases, with children in the larger families being less likely to be enrolled than those from 0-1-2 sibling families. The education of the mother and father has a positive and significant effect, and their magnitudes are identical. A decrease in the mother's education or the father's education below the mean to 8 years reduces the probability of enrollment from 0.76 to 0.69, and an increase in the level of the mother's education or the father's education above the mean to 18 years increases the probability of enrollment to 0.83. Finally, net income (household income minus teenagers' own earnings) has a positive impact on school enrollment, thus implying that students from low income families are more likely to drop out of high school relative to their counterparts from middle and high income families. However, the partial effect of income on the enrollment probability is much weaker compared to the 3 to 5 age group. An increase in income from $30,000 to $70,000 changes the probability of enrollment from 0.75 to 0.77. This weaker effect of income on high school enrollment relative to preschool enrollment can be attributed to public high school education being tuition free. Family income, however, has more of an indirect impact on teenage enrollment – it serves as an indicator for other social and economic factors that are likely to impact a teenager's decision to stay/drop out of high school.

The second specification (column 2 of table 22A) added the birthplace dummy variables to the usual explanatory variables. The benchmark was native-parentage children age 16 to 18 years, hence the coefficients represent the difference in enrollment between first-generation teenagers from a particular country and their native-parentage counterparts. Inclusion of the country-of-origin dummy variables had a limited impact on the magnitudes or statistical significance of most of the variables in the original estimating equation. The variable Hispanic is now statistically significant. Among the country coefficients that are significant, South Asians depict the highest probability of being enrolled, followed by East Asians, Chinese, Middle Easterners, and Southern Europeans. The probability of school enrollment (column 2 in table 22B) increases from 0.76 for native-parentage, to 0.96 for immigrant children from South Asia, and to 0.93 for immigrant children from East Asia, China, and Vietnam.

School Enrollment of First-Generation Children

This section discusses the sample of 3,560 first-generation 16- to 18-year-old children. Table 23 depicts the means and standard deviations of school enrollment by country-of-origin. As column 2 indicates, approximately 7% of immigrants are from English-speaking countries

TABLE 23. SUMMARY STATISTICS BY COUNTRY-OF-ORIGIN, FIRST-GENERATION CHILDREN, UNITED STATES, 1990

AGE GROUP 16 TO 18 YEARS

Country-of-Origin	Sample Size	Percent of all Foreign-Born	Enrollment
English-speaking countries	254	7.13	0.92 (0.28)[a]
Africa	43	1.21	0.91 (0.29)
Mexico	1,021	28.28	0.81 (0.39)
Cuba	87	2.44	0.91 (0.29)
S. & C. America	388	10.90	0.91 (0.28)
Caribbean	95	2.67	0.97 (0.18)
Southern Europe	90	2.53	0.89 (0.31)
E. & C. Europe	160	4.49	0.92 (0.28)
N. & W. Europe	19	0.53	0.84 (0.36)
Philippines	213	5.98	0.92 (0.27)
China	100	2.81	0.93 (0.25)
Vietnam	286	8.03	0.93 (0.25)
East Asia	258	7.25	0.95 (0.22)
South Asia	131	3.68	0.99 (0.05)
Middle East	114	3.20	0.91 (0.28)
Other Asia	226	6.35	0.94 (0.24)
Remaining countries	75	2.11	0.88 (0.32)
Total	3,560	100.00	0.90 (0.31)

Source: 1990 Census of Population of United States, Public Use Microdata Sample, 1% file.

Note: Variables are as defined in Table 29 in appendix.
[a] standard errors for all variables are indicated in parentheses.

(United Kingdom, England, Australia, New Zealand, British West Indies). The dominant immigrant source country is Mexico (above 30%), followed by South and Central America (11%), and East Asia (7%). Column 3 indicates that immigrant children from South Asia (99%), followed by immigrant children from the Caribbean (97%), clearly have the highest enrollment rates, while immigrant children from Southern Europe (89%), North and West Europe (84%), and Mexico (81%) have the lowest enrollment rates. These findings are not surprising given our earlier results on educational attainment that indicated consistently high education levels for immigrants from South and East Asia, and low levels for immigrants from Mexico and Southern Europe. The enrollment rate is between 91% and 94% for all the other country groups.

Probit results for the first-generation sample are summarized in Table 24, A and B. The dependent variable for the probit equation was 'school enrollment.' As in the analysis of the pooled sample, two different specifications were considered. The benchmark age group in the probit equation is 16 years and the benchmark age-at-immigration group is those immigrating between 0 and 4 years. The discussion here focuses on the probit coefficients and predicted probabilities. Corresponding marginal effects are reported in Table 40, Appendix. Model (1) of the probit for the first-generation sample (column 1 of table 24A) depicts that only a few variables are statistically significant. The negative coefficient of the age dummy variables reflects that the probability of dropping out of high school increases with age. The reference group in the calculation of the foreign-born sample's predicted probability of high school enrollment is an 18-year-old male immigrant from an English-speaking country with age-at-immigration less than 4 years. The probability of being enrolled in high school drops from 0.88 for children with good English proficiency to 0.64 for those with poor English proficiency. The negative coefficient of the Hispanic variable reveals that Hispanic students are more likely than their non-Hispanic counterparts to drop out of high school. The low enrollment rates among first-generation Hispanic teenagers have two underlying reasons. One, large numbers of Hispanics who immigrate in their teenage years do not enroll in high school upon arrival in the United States. Two, home resources that are believed to have a strong positive impact on the incidence of dropping out is particularly weak for first-generation Hispanics due to their parents' lower socioeconomic status and limited English speaking ability. Both the geographic variables are significant – while residence in the South has a positive effect,

TABLE 24A. PROBIT ESTIMATES OF FIRST-GENERATION CHILDREN, UNITED STATES, 1990

DEPENDENT VARIABLE: SCHOOL ENROLLMENT

AGE GROUP 16 TO 18 YEARS

Variable	(1)	(2)[a]
Constant	0.589	0.494
	(3.68)	(2.09)
Male	-0.112	-0.113
	(1.83)	(1.82)
Age17	-0.280	-0.293
	(3.45)	(3.58)
Age18	-0.545	-0.539
	(6.66)	(6.48)
Black	-0.022	-0.089
	(0.14)	(0.46)
Hispanic	-0.335	-0.158
	(4.70)	(0.89)
South	0.168	0.166
	(2.23)	(2.12)
Rural	-0.318	-0.286
	(2.97)	(2.61)
English proficiency	0.842	0.869
	(9.58)	(9.67)
Mother's education	0.014	0.015
	(1.46)	(1.54)
Father's education	0.022	0.017
	(2.43)	(1.85)
Mother works full-time	0.025	0.033
	(0.37)	(0.48)
Mother works part-time	-0.166	-0.155
	(1.69)	(1.56)
1 Sibling	0.204	0.200
	(2.43)	(2.33)
2 Siblings	0.115	0.110
	(1.30)	(1.20)
3 Siblings	0.220	0.223
	(1.91)	(1.87)
4+ Siblings	0.077	0.108
	(0.69)	(0.93)
Net income	1.14e-06	1.45e-06
	(1.08)	(1.33)

TABLE 24A (continued)

Variable	(1)	(2)[a]
Age-at-immigration 5 to 12	0.018	-0.028
	(0.23)	(0.34)
Age-at-immigration 13 to 18	-0.044	-0.094
	(0.49)	(1.02)
BIRTHPLACE		
Africa	n.e.	-0.007
		(0.02)
Mexico	n.e.	-0.122
		(0.53)
Cuba	n.e.	-0.113
		(0.40)
S. & C. America	n.e.	0.082
		(0.37)
Caribbean	n.e.	0.901
		(2.62)
Southern Europe	n.e.	-0.109
		(0.45)
E. & C. Europe	n.e.	0.066
		(0.30)
N. & W. Europe	n.e.	-0.533
		(1.36)
Philippines	n.e.	-0.120
		(0.59)
China	n.e.	0.300
		(1.17)
Vietnam	n.e.	0.277
		(1.36)
East Asia	n.e.	0.328
		(1.35)
South Asia	n.e.	0.804
		(2.06)
Middle East	n.e.	-0.020
		(0.08)
Other Asia	n.e.	0.276
		(1.29)
Remaining countries	n.e.	-0.211
		(0.83)
Pseudo R^2	0.140	0.156
Sample size	3,560	3,560

Source: 1990 Census of Population of United States, Public Use Microdata Sample, 1% file.

Note: Variables are as defined in Table 29 in appendix.
  n.e. = Variable not entered. t statistics are in parentheses.
  [a] benchmark group is all first-generation 16 to 18 year age group children from English-speaking countries.

TABLE 24B. PREDICTED PROBABILITIES OF SCHOOL ENROLLMENT FOR FIRST-GENERATION CHILDREN, UNITED STATES, 1990

AGE GROUP 16 TO 18 YEARS

Reference child[a]	0.88	Reference child[b]	0.87
Female	0.90	Africa	0.86
Age16	0.96*	Mexico	0.84
Age17	0.93*	Cuba	0.84
Black	0.88	S. & C. America	0.88
Hispanic	0.80*	Caribbean	0.98*
South	0.91*	Southern Europe	0.84
Rural	0.81*	E. & C. Europe	0.88
Not English proficient	0.64*	N. & W. Europe	0.72
Age-at-immigration 5 to 12	0.89	Philippines	0.84
Age-at-immigration 13 to 18	0.87	China	0.92
1 Sibling	0.92*	Vietnam	0.92
2 Siblings	0.90	East Asia	0.92
3 Siblings	0.92	South Asia	0.97*
4+ Siblings	0.90	Middle East	0.86
Mother works full-time	0.89	Other Asia	0.92
Mother works part-time	0.85		
Mother's education (mean=9.65)			
8	0.88		
12	0.89		
16	0.90		
18	0.91		

TABLE 24B (continued)

Reference child[a]	0.88	Reference child[b]	0.87
Father's education (mean=10.53)			
8	0.87*		
12	0.89*		
16	0.91*		
18	0.91*		
Net income (mean = 41,794)			
10,000	0.88		
20,000	0.88		
50,000	0.89		
60,000	0.92		

Source: Table 24A

Reference child is a 16-year-old male (non-black, non-Hispanic) immigrant (age-at-immigration 0 to 4) from an English-speaking country with a non-working mother and no siblings, residing in an urban, non-south region with mean values for the continuous variables.

Note: [a] based on column (1) of Table 24A.
[b] based on column (2) of Table 24A.
* implies that estimated coefficients of the probit model were significant.

residence in rural areas has a negative effect on the probability of high school enrollment. The mother's education, mother's labor force participation, and net income are statistically insignificant. The father's education, on the other hand, has a positive impact on the probability of high school enrollment of the 16- to 18-year-old first-generation immigrants. The probability of school enrollment increases from 0.87 to 0.91 for an increase in father's education from 8 years to 18 years. Teenagers with one sibling have higher probability of being enrolled in high school than those with no siblings, but none of the other sibling dummy variables are significant.

The second specification (column 2 in table 24A) added the birthplace dummy variables to the usual explanatory variables. The benchmark group was first-generation children from English-speaking countries in the 16 to 18 age group. Inclusion of the country-of-origin dummy variables makes two of the original explanatory variables, Hispanic and father's education, statistically insignificant.[22] The only birthplace coefficients that are significant[23] are South Asia and the Caribbean, both of which have a positive association with school enrollment. Immigrant children from South Asia and the Caribbean have a 97% probability of school enrollment compared to an 87% probability of enrollment for immigrant children from English-speaking countries.

Comparative Study of First-Generation, Second-Generation, and Native-Parentage Children

Probits estimated separately for first-generation, second-generation, and native-parentage children are presented in Table 25, Parts A and B. Corresponding marginal effects are reported in Table 41, Appendix. This section focuses not on the individual sample probit coefficients but rather discusses some of the more important differences in the factors affecting school enrollment among the first-generation, second-generation, and native-parentage. A comparison of the probit for the first- and second-generation with the native-parentage children reveals that most of the variables that were significant in the probit equation for native-parentage children lose their significance in the probit equation for second-generation and first-generation. The variables, Hispanic and English proficiency, have a negative and positive effect, respectively, on school enrollment for first-generation children, but have no impact either on second-generation or on native-parentage children. In contrast to the strong effect of both the mother's and father's education in the native-parentage sample probit, only the father's education is of significance (though much weaker) in the first-generation sample. The only variables significant in the second-generation probit for the 16 to 18 age group are the mother and father's education, though the impact is less pronounced compared to the native-parentage children. Moreover, the sibling variables seem to be more important in enrollment decisions among the native-parentage children.

We introduced three variables: mother-only foreign-born, father-only foreign-born, and both parents foreign-born in a specification combining all the second-generation and native-parentage children. These variables should capture the effect, if any, of U.S.-born children having foreign-born versus native-born parents. The probability of

TABLE 25A. PROBIT ESTIMATES OF SECOND-GENERATION AND NATIVE-PARENTAGE CHILDREN, UNITED STATES, 1990

DEPENDENT VARIABLE: SCHOOL ENROLLMENT

AGE GROUP 16 TO 18 YEARS

Variable	Second-Generation	Native-Parentage	All Native-Born
Constant	0.936 (4.75)	-0.024 (0.24)	0.079 (0.87)
Male	0.016 (0.32)	-0.068 (4.44)	-0.062 (4.28)
Age17	-0.285 (4.17)	-0.202 (9.62)	-0.209 (10.46)
Age18	-0.733 (10.82)	-0.861 (42.59)	-0.849 (43.92)
Black	-0.152 (1.20)	0.094 (3.30)	0.068 (2.46)
Hispanic	0.005 (0.07)	0.024 (0.64)	0.077 (2.42)
South	0.031 (0.52)	-0.041 (2.52)	-0.035 (2.25)
Rural	-0.153 (2.29)	0.093 (5.77)	0.076 (4.89)
English proficiency	0.227 (1.43)	-0.011 (0.12)	0.066 (0.86)
Mother's education	0.021 (2.42)	0.069 (16.61)	0.059 (15.66)
Father's education	0.026 (3.29)	0.054 (16.20)	0.049 (16.10)
Mother works full-time	0.013 (0.22)	0.030 (1.71)	0.033 (1.93)
Mother works part-time	0.002 (0.075)	0.109 (4.89)	0.105 (4.93)
1 Sibling	0.019 (0.29)	0.134 (6.85)	0.126 (6.75)
2 Siblings	0.064 (0.80)	0.067 (2.56)	0.071 (2.86)
3 Siblings	-0.066 (0.61)	0.006 (0.14)	0.003 (0.09)
4+ Siblings	-0.060 (0.46)	-0.143 (3.00)	-0.124 (2.77)
Net income	1.20e-06 (1.63)	1.79e-06 (6.57)	1.81e-06 (7.04)
Mother foreign-born	n.e.	n.e.	0.183 (3.69)
Father foreign-born	n.e.	n.e.	0.113 (2.12)
Both parents foreign-born	n.e.	n.e.	0.507 (11.38)
Sample size	5,401	56,757	62,158

Source: 1990 Census of Population of United States, Public Use Microdata Sample, 1% file.

Note: Variables are as defined in Table 29 in appendix.

n.e. = Variable not entered. t statistics are in parentheses.

TABLE 25B. PREDICTED PROBABILITIES OF SECOND-GENERATION AND NATIVE –PARENTAGE CHILDREN, UNITED STATES, 1990

AGE GROUP <u>16 TO 18</u> YEARS

	Second-Generation	Native-Parentage	All Native-Born
Reference child	0.87[a]	0.77[b]	0.76[c]
Female	0.86	0.79*	0.78*
Age16	0.97*	0.94*	0.94*
Age17	0.94*	0.93*	0.91*
Black	0.83	0.79*	0.78*
Hispanic	0.87	0.77	0.79*
South	0.87	0.75*	0.75*
Rural	0.83*	0.79*	0.79*
Not English proficient	0.81	0.77	0.74
1 Sibling	0.87	0.80*	0.80*
2 Siblings	0.88	0.79*	0.78*
3 Siblings	0.85	0.77	0.76
4+ Siblings	0.85	0.72*	0.72*
Mother works full-time	0.87	0.77	0.77
Mother works part-time	0.87	0.80*	0.79*
Mother foreign-born	n.e.	n.e.	0.84*
Father foreign-born	n.e.	n.e.	0.83*
Both parents foreign-born	n.e.	n.e.	0.91*

TABLE 25B (continued)

	Second-Generation	Native-Parentage	All Native-Born
Reference child	0.87[a]	0.77[b]	0.76[c]
Mother's education (mean=11.34[d];12.90[e];12.77[f])			
8	0.84*	0.65*	0.67*
10	0.85*	0.70*	0.71*
16	0.88*	0.83*	0.82*
18	0.89*	0.86*	0.85*
Father's education (mean=11.70d[c];13.12[e];13.00[f])			
8	0.84*	0.67*	0.68*
10	0.85*	0.71*	0.72*
16	0.88*	0.81*	0.81*
18	0.89*	0.84*	0.83*
Net income (mean=55283[d];52239[e];52503f[c])			
10,000	0.85	0.74*	0.74*
20,000	0.86	0.75*	0.75*
50,000	0.87	0.76*	0.76*
60,000	0.87	0.77*	0.77*

Source: Table 25A

Reference child is an 18-year-old native white male with a non-working mother and no siblings, residing in an urban, non-south region with mean values for the continuous variables.

Note: [a] based on columns (1) of Table 25 A.
　　[b] based on columns (3) of Table 25 A.
　　[c] based on columns (3) of Table 25 A.
　　[d] means for second-generation; [e] means for native-parentage; [f] means for all native-born.
　　* implies that estimated coefficients of the probit model were significant.

school enrollment increases from 0.76 for children with both parents native-born, to 0.84 for children with mother-only foreign-born, to 0.83 for father-only foreign-born, and to 0.91 for children with both parents foreign-born. The strong positive effect of having both parents foreign-born was also found by Schultz (1984).

In general, estimates for probit run separately for males and females are very similar to each other and to those run for the entire adult sample. Since they do not contribute significantly to this present study, the results are not reported or discussed.

EMPIRICAL ANALYSIS OF THE OCTOBER 1995 CPS DATA

This section discusses the analysis conducted in the previous section in the context of the October CPS dataset. The CPS dataset did not enable us to replicate the Census data analysis. First, there was no usable information to construct two variables important to our analysis, namely, number of siblings and English proficiency. Second, due to the much smaller size of the CPS dataset, it was econometrically difficult to study the different country-of-origin subgroups. Third, the CPS asked school enrollment questions to three distinct populations: 3 to 5 years, 6 to 14 years, and 15 years and older. Given this nature of the enrollment question, the high school-related analysis using the CPS data was conducted on the 15 to 18 age group.

School Enrollment of First-Generation, Second-Generation, and Native-Parentage Children

This section discusses the results for the pooled sample of 4,949 first-generation, second-generation, and native-parentage 15- to 18-year-old children. Comparative statistics for first-generation, second-generation, and native-parentage children for the two age groups are summarized in Table 26. For the 15- to 18-year-olds, school enrollment is highest among second-generation (96%), followed by the native-parentage (93%), and first-generation (88%) children. The distribution of blacks/non-blacks and Hispanics/non-Hispanics is very similar to the 3 to 5 age group. Similar to the Census results, the average level of education of both parents increases by a year between the first- and second-generation, and by more than a year between the second-generation and native-parentage children. With each subsequent generation, the percentage of mothers working also goes up, and as can be expected, the mother's labor force participation increases substantially in the 15 to 18 age group compared to the 3 to 5 age group.

Table 27, Parts A and B summarize the probit results for the pooled sample. Corresponding marginal effects are reported in Appendix, Table 42. The dependent variable for the probit equation was 'school enrollment'. Two different specifications were considered. The primary explanatory variables used in both specifications were male, black, Hispanic, South, non-MSA, household income, mother and father's education level, mother's labor force participation and dummy variables for age. The basic specification (column 1 in table 27A) simply used the above-mentioned set of demographic and geographic variables as the explanatory variables, and added variables first-generation, second-generation, and age-at-immigration dummy variables to capture the effects of immigrant generation and age-at-immigration. Most of the explanatory variables in model (1) of the probit for the total 16 to 18 age group pooled sample are statistically significant. As found in the Census analysis, school enrollment clearly falls with age, with a particularly big drop for 18-year-olds. The positive coefficient on second-generation implies that second-generation immigrants have a higher probability of being enrolled in high school relative to their native counterparts. The probability of enrollment increases from 0.66 for native-parentage to 0.85 for second-generation. Neither the variable first-generation nor the age-at-immigration dummy variables are statistically significant. Being black is also associated with a higher enrollment probability (0.78 compared to 0.66 for a white child). The mother's labor supply variables have a positive and significant impact on school enrollment – the probability of enrollment increases from 0.66 to 0.74 if the mother works part-time or full-time. Consistent with our analysis so far, the higher the mother's education and the father's education, the more likely is a teenager to be enrolled in high school. While family income has a positive influence on the probability of high school enrollment, the effect is not as strong as for the 3 to 5 age group.

TABLE 26. SUMMARY STATISTICS OF VARIABLES, BY FIRST-GENERATION, SECOND-GENERATION, AND NATIVE-PARENTAGE CHILDREN, UNITED STATES, 1995

AGE GROUP 15 TO 18 YEARS

Variable	First-Generation	Second-Generation	Native-Parentage
School enrollment	0.88	0.96	0.93
	(0.32)	(0.21)	(0.26)
Male	0.48	0.54	0.51
	(0.50)	(0.50)	(0.50)
Age	16.43	16.41	16.4
	(1.22)	(1.11)	(1.11)
Age-at-immigration	7.62	n.a.	n.a.
	(4.88)		
Black	0.06	0.05	0.10
	(0.24)	(0.22)	(0.30)
Hispanic	0.50	0.42	0.03
	(0.50)	(0.49)	(0.17)
South	0.28	0.26	0.35
	(0.45)	(0.44)	(0.48)
Non-MSA	0.93	0.89	0.72
	(0.25)	(032)	(0.45)
Mother's education	10.23	11.84	13.35
	(4.73)	(3.68)	(2.16)
Father's education	10.85	12.04	13.68
	(4.45)	(4.49)	(2.52)
Mother works full-time	0.45	0.48	0.54
	(0.50)	(0.50)	(0.50)
Mother works part-time	0.10	0.16	0.22
	(0.30)	(0.36)	(0.42)
Mother not working	0.44	0.36	0.24
	(0.50)	(0.48)	0.43
Household income	28310	41023	46119
	(23905)	(28780)	(28247)
Sample size	256	532	4,161

Source: October 1995 Current Population Survey, United States Census Bureau.

Note: Variables are as defined in Table 29 in appendix.
   n.a. = Variable not applicable.
   standard errors for all variables are in parentheses.

TABLE 27A. PROBIT ESTIMATES OF POOLED SAMPLE OF FIRST-GENERATION, SECOND-GENERATION, AND NATIVE-PARENTAGE CHILDREN, UNITED STATES, 1995

DEPENDENT VARIABLE: SCHOOL ENROLLMENT

AGE GROUP 15 TO 18 YEARS

Variable	(1)
Constant	-0.052 (0.25)
Male	-0.130 (2.00)
Age15	0.468 (3.50)
Age17	-0.218 (2.16)
Age18	-1.296 (14.61)
Black	0.345 (2.56)
Hispanic	-0.053 (0.40)
South	-0.065 (0.89)
Non-MSA	0.200 (2.68)
First-generation	0.437 (1.89)
Second-generation	0.638 (4.56)
Age-at-immigration 5 to 12	0.151 (0.51)
Age-at-immigration 13 to 18	-0.207 (0.65)
Household income	6.73e-06 (4.90)
Mother's education	0.068 (4.09)
Father's education	0.052 (3.57)
Mother works full-time	0.220 (2.87)
Mother works part-time	0.223 (2.35)
Pseudo R^2	0.267
Sample size	4,949

Source: October 1995 Current Population Survey, United States Census Bureau.

Note: Variables are as defined in Table 29 in appendix.
   n.e. = Variable not entered.   t statistics are in parentheses.

TABLE 27B. PREDICTED PROBABILITIES OF SCHOOL ENROLLMENT FOR POOLED SAMPLE, UNITED STATES, 1995

AGE GROUP 15 TO 18 YEARS

Reference child[a]	0.66
Female	0.71*
Age15	0.99*
Age16	0.96*
Age17	0.93*
Black	0.78*
Hispanic	0.64
South	0.72
Non-MSA	0.58*
First-generation	0.80
Second-generation	0.85*
Age-at-immigration 5 to 12	0.64
Age-at-immigration 13 to 18	0.73
Mother works full-time	0.74*
Mother works part-time	0.74*
Mother's education (mean = 13.13)	
8	0.52*
10	0.58*
16	0.73*
18	0.77*

TABLE 27B (continued)

Reference child[a]	**0.66**

Father's education (mean = 13.42)	
8	0.55*
10	0.59*
16	0.71*
18	0.74*
Household income (mean = 44,934)	
10,000	0.57*
20,000	0.60*
60,000	0.70*
70,000	0.72*

Source: Table 27A

Reference child is an 18-year-old native white male with a non-working mother and no siblings, residing in a metropolitan, non-south region with mean values for the continuous variables.

Note: [a] based on column (1) of Table 27 Part A.
          * implies that estimated coefficients of the probit model were significant.

Comparative Study of First-Generation, Second-Generation, and Native-Parentage Children

Probits estimated separately for the first-generation, second-generation, and native-parentage children are presented in Table 28, Parts A and B. Corresponding marginal effects are reported in Appendix, Table 43. For this age group, when estimating the probit model for the second-generation, two variables, black and non-MSA, were dropped because they predicted the outcome perfectly. The observations that led to the problem were eliminated so as not to bias the remaining coefficients in the model. However, due to the larger sample size of the second-generation sample, estimation was successful. A comparison of the probit for the first- and second-generation with the native-parentage children reveals that all the variables that were significant in the probit equation for native-parentage lose their significance in the probit equation for second-generation and first-generation. In fact, while black, non-MSA, family income, parental education, and mother's labor supply variables were significant in the native-parentage sample, none of them retain their significance in either immigrant generation sample.

In order to examine the effect of foreign-parentage on the high school enrollment patterns of U.S.-born children, we introduce three variables: mother-only foreign-born, father-only foreign-born, and both parents foreign-born in a specification combining the second-generation and native-parentage children. Having only the mother foreign-born as well as having both parents foreign-born has a positive impact on enrollment.

DISCUSSION

Among teenagers, high school enrollment clearly falls with age – in other words, dropout rates typically increase after age 16, since in most states mandatory school attendance is required until the age of 16. Teenage males have a lower probability of being enrolled in high school than do females, and teenagers with lower English proficiency have a higher probability of dropping out of high school compared to those with good English proficiency. The probability that a teenage youth is enrolled in school is higher if he is a first- or second-generation immigrant. The probability of high school enrollment is also higher for children with working mothers, confirming most research that points to the positive impacts of the mother working as a child grows older. Both the mother's education and the father's education are equally important in determining the probability of high school enrollment of children. Relative to native-parentage children, the probability of enrollment is higher for immigrants from South and East Asia, the Middle East, and Southern Europe. Hirschman (2001), who investigated educational enrollment of 15 to 17-year-old immigrants to the United States, also found that non-enrollment is very low among youths born in Asia. In fact, Asian youths are more likely to be in school than are native-born youths. He found that non-enrollment rates are highest among immigrants from Mexico, Puerto Rico, Cuba, the Dominican Republic, El Salvador, and Guatemala. While groups from the Hispanic Caribbean have high non-enrollment rates, those from the

TABLE 28A. PROBIT ESTIMATES OF SECOND-GENERATION AND NATIVE-PARENTAGE CHILDREN, UNITED STATES, 1995

DEPENDENT VARIABLE: SCHOOL ENROLLMENT

AGE GROUP 15 TO 18 YEARS

Variable	Second-Generation	Native-Parentage	All Native-Born
Constant	1.364	-0.787	-0.513
	(2.37)	(2.95)	(2.15)
Male	0.111	-0.111	-0.085
	(0.46)	(1.55)	(1.25)
Age15	dropped	0.410	0.470
		(2.80)	(3.33)
Age17	0.129	-0.265	-0.219
	(0.35)	(2.35)	(2.07)
Age18	-1.013	-1.377	-1.323
	(3.48)	(13.73)	(14.16)
Black	dropped	0.330	0.340
		(2.36)	(2.48)
Hispanic	-0.431	-0.004	-0.056
	(1.50)	(0.02)	(0.38)
South	-0.085	-0.020	-0.027
	(0.27)	(0.25)	(0.35)
Non-MSA	dropped	0.220	0.235
		(2.80)	(3.06)
Household income	4.21e-06	6.45e-06	6.52e-06
	(0.80)	(4.25)	(4.53)
Mother's education	-0.028	0.114	0.094
	(0.55)	(5.41)	(4.91)
Father's education	0.076	0.067	0.062
	(1.71)	(3.78)	(3.87)
Mother works full-time	-0.061	0.218	0.199
	(0.21)	(2.54)	(2.45)
Mother works part-time	-0.082	0.228	0.219
	(0.19)	(2.21)	(2.21)
Mother foreign-born	n.e.	n.e.	0.822
			(2.65)
Father foreign-born	n.e.	n.e.	0.266
			(1.27)
Both parents foreign-born	n.e.	n.e.	1.013
			(4.84)
Pseudo R^2	0.223	0.284	0.280
Sample size	310	4,161	4,693

Source: October 1995 Current Population Survey, United States Census Bureau.

Note: Variables are as defined in Table 29 in appendix.
n.e. = Variable not entered. t statistics are in parentheses.

TABLE 28B. PREDICTED PROBABILITIES OF SECOND-GENERATION AND NATIVE-PARENTAGE CHILDREN, UNITED STATES, 1995

AGE GROUP 15 TO 18 YEARS

	Second-Generation	Native-Parentage	All Native-Born
Reference child	0.89^a	0.68^b	0.68^c
Female	0.87	0.72	0.71
Age15	-	0.99*	0.99
Age16	0.99	0.97*	0.96*
Age17	0.99*	0.94*	0.94*
Black	-	0.79*	0.79*
Hispanic	0.79	0.68	0.65
South	0.88	0.67	0.67
Non-MSA	-	0.75	0.75*
Mother works full-time	0.88	0.75*	0.74*
Mother works part-time	0.87	0.76*	0.75*
Mother foreign-born	n.e.	n.e.	0.93*
Father foreign-born	n.e.	n.e.	0.83
Both parents foreign-born	n.e.	n.e.	0.95*
Mother's education (mean=12.12^d;13.40^e;13.26^f)			
8	0.91	0.44*	0.49*
10	0.90	0.53*	0.56*
16	0.87	0.78*	0.76*
18	0.86	0.84*	0.82*

TABLE 28B (continued)

	Second-Generation	Native-Parentage	All Native-Born
Reference child	0.89[a]	0.68[b]	0.68[c]
Father's education (mean=12.43[d];13.70[e];13.55[f])			
8	0.82	0.54*	0.54*
10	0.85	0.59*	0.59*
16	0.93	0.73*	0.73*
18	0.95	0.78*	0.77*
Household income: (mean=42,878[d]; 46,221[e];45,793[f])			
10,000	0.86	0.59*	0.59*
20,000	0.87	0.62*	0.61*
60,000	0.90	0.71*	0.71*

Source: Table 28A

Reference child is an 18-year-old native white male with a non-working mother and no siblings, residing in a metropolitan, non-south region with mean values for the continuous variables.

Note: [a] based on column (1) of Table 28A;
[b] based on column (3) of Table 28A;
[c] based on   column (3) of Table 28A.
[d] means for second-generation, [e] means for native-parentage, [f] means for all native-born.
* implies that estimated coefficients of the probit model were significant.

West Indies (Haiti, Jamaica) are at par with native-borns. Thus, dropping out of school is a problem for a few national-origin groups.

In comparing the determinants of school enrollment across first-generation, second-generation, and native-parentage children, we find once again that the effect of the mother and father's education is most pronounced for native-parentage children followed by second-generation children. Importantly, the mother's education seems to have no effect on the first-generation – a result that is not surprising given

Gang and Zimmerman's (1999) finding that parental education has no impact on the educational attainment of first-generation immigrants to Germany. For U.S.-born children, our results indicate that having one or both parents foreign-born has a positive impact on enrollment probability relative to having both parents native-born. The only birthplace coefficients significant in the first-generation sample were South Asia and the Caribbean, both of which are associated with higher enrollment rates relative to their counterparts from English-speaking countries.

CHAPTER 8

CONCLUSION

Given the importance of immigrants in the U.S. workforce and the increasing awareness of the critical role of education in labor market success, this study sought to investigate the determinants of the school enrollment and educational attainment of immigrants. This work contributes to the existing literature on education by examining the educational aspect of the assimilation process of immigrants, through the separate investigation by first-generation and second-generation immigrants, and analysis among immigrants by age-at-immigration and country-of-origin.

MAJOR FINDINGS

This study clearly exhibits that educational attainment, preschool enrollment, and high school enrollment differ significantly among first-generation, second-generation, and native-parentage immigrants.

The immigrant generation analysis shows that second-generation immigrants acquire about half a year more schooling than their native-parentage counterparts. Other explanatory variables (age, gender, marital status) held constant, first-generation immigrants who immigrate at a very young age (up to age 5) acquire 0.35 years more schooling than second-generation, and 0.81 years more schooling than native-parentage adults. However, immigration from age 5 up to age 19 is associated with lesser schooling than second-generation immigrants, and immigration from age 13 up to age 19 is associated with fewer years of schooling even relative to native-parentage adults. Immigration in the teenage years thus conveys the greatest disadvantage. Those who migrate late in their twenties complete more schooling (about half a year) than those migrating in their teen years. However, the attainment level drops significantly and progressively with age-at-immigration beyond 30. Thus the empirical analysis supports the hypothesis regarding the negative effect of age-at-immigration on post-migration investment in schooling, but the estimated relationship is complex, with a big dip among those who immigrate as teenagers. The analysis also indicates that being black, and more so being Hispanic, is associated with lower levels of education compared to non-Hispanic whites for immigrants, second-generation, and native-parentage adults. The black/non-black differential is less than a year but the Hispanic/non-Hispanic differential is typically more than two years. While the Hispanic/non-Hispanic differential is less pronounced with each subsequent generation, the black/non-black differential persists, and in fact, is strongest in the native-parentage generation.

The analysis of preschool enrollment (age 3 to 5 years) by immigrant generation reflects that other variables (age, family size, parental education) held constant, and both first-generation and second-generation children are 5 to 10 percent more likely to be enrolled in preschool than their native-parentage counterparts. Among two-parent households the determinants of preschool enrollment differ significantly among the three immigrant generations.

The two variables intended to capture minority group effects (black and Hispanic) impact school enrollment differently for the three immigrant generations. Being black does not affect the probability of preschool enrollment among first-generation children. But among second-generation and native-parentage children, blacks are about 7 percent more likely than non-blacks to enroll in preschool. Being Hispanic, on the other hand, has no impact on the enrollment probability of native-parentage children, but lowers the probability of enrollment of first-generation and second-generation children by about 5 percent.

The positive role of parental education in preschool enrollment is somewhat stronger among native-parentage children relative to either first-generation or second-generation children. Moreover, the mother's labor force participation has no effect on preschool enrollment decisions of first-generation children, a small effect on preschool enrollment decisions of second-generation children, and the strongest impact on native-parentage children's preschool enrollment.

Very few variables are significant in explaining high school enrollment (age 16 to 18 years) for first-generation and second-generation immigrants. In general, however, first-generation and second-generation children show a 10 to 12 percent higher probability of enrollment relative to their native counterparts. Among first-generation children, Hispanic teenagers are 8 percent less likely than non-Hispanic teenagers to be enrolled in high school, and teenagers who are not English proficient are 20 percent less likely than English-proficient teenagers to be enrolled in high school. Among native-parentage children, males have a lower probability of being enrolled in high school than females, but this gender differential is not observed for the other two generation groups. While parental education has a strong positive role in determining high school enrollment of native-parentage children, and a weaker effect for second-generation children, only the father's education matters in enrollment of first-generation children.

Another major finding of this study is the substantial heterogeneity that exists among immigrants depending on their country-of-origin and age-at-immigration. Immigrants from Africa, South and East Asia, the Philippines, and North and West Europe obtain 1 to 1.5 years more schooling in comparison to their counterparts born in the U.S. or immigrants from English-speaking countries. Mexicans and Southern Europeans, on the other hand, achieve less schooling relative to the native-born adults, as well as immigrants from English-speaking countries. Mexicans lag behind their U.S.-born and English-speaking birthplace immigrant counterparts about 4 years. The lower education of Mexican immigrants can be attributed to the nature of migration from Mexico to the United States, a large percentage being illegal immigrants who have less economic incentive to invest in human capital. Additionally, given the close proximity of Mexico to the United States, cost of to-and fro-migration is very low, and this factor leads to a weaker incentive to invest in both origin-specific and destination-specific skills.

The probit analysis of school enrollment demonstrates that immigrant children from Mexico, the Caribbean, East and Central Europe, South Asia, and the Middle East have a lower probability of being enrolled in preschool than their immigrant counterparts from English-speaking developed countries. At the same time, immigrant teenagers from South Asia and the Caribbean are more likely to be enrolled in high school relative to their English-speaking counterparts. While age-at-immigration is not of any significance in explaining preschool enrollment, immigrating in the teenage years does lower the probability of being enrolled in high school.

Overall, the results described here demonstrate that educational attainment of adults as well as school enrollment of children varies by immigrant generation, by country-of-origin, and by age-at-immigration. Also, among adults born in the U.S., having one or both parents foreign-born has a positive effect on educational attainment relative to those having both parents native-born. In the enrollment analysis, other variables held constant, and household income has a strong positive association with the probability of being enrolled in school, though its effect on high school enrollment is weaker relative to its effect on preschool enrollment. The sign, magnitude, and significance of the sibling variable varies among the different immigrant generations, and hence the effect of family size (as proxied by number of siblings) on school enrollment is not clear from this analysis.

POLICY IMPLICATIONS

The policy implications of our findings are significant, particularly for the minority groups studied. Some of our findings are similar to past studies that indicate that intergenerational effects persist (Dicks and Sweetman, 1999; Chiswick, 1988). Also evident from our analysis is that blacks and Hispanics continue to lag behind in their schooling acquisition, which confirms earlier studies (Vernez and Abrahmse, 1996) that a growing share of the student population is lagging behind the rest in educational attainment. Therefore, it seems appropriate to enact immigration, assimilation, and education policies to not only prevent this existing educational gap from widening any further, but also to narrow the existing gap over the next few years.

Two kinds of policy can be used to influence the education levels of the immigrant population. First, immigration policy can be used to reduce the existing gap among various ethnic groups by restricting immigration among adults to those with some specified minimum level of schooling. Also, first-generation and second-generation immigrants are likely to have more favorable labor market outcomes if immigration policy is used to promote immigration by younger people with a relatively high education level and reasonable knowledge of destination language. Education plays a critical role in the economic assimilation of immigrants since it paves the way for their labor market success in the destination country. Labor market success of immigrants, on the other hand, is used to evaluate the success of immigration policy.

Since the pace of assimilation of immigrants affects the rate of human capital accumulation of immigrant children (Djajic, 2003), policies that help immigrants in assimilation will also affect the investment in human capital of the second-generation. Therefore, assimilation policy can be used to help immigrants, adults as well as children, to assimilate into the host country, particularly in overcoming language and education barriers. Our analysis indicates that racial/ethnic differences are most prominent in the first-generation among Hispanics. For example, assimilation policy involving increased commitment to the education of immigrants through emphasis on the acquisition of language skills can play a major role in facilitating the adjustment and progress of Hispanic immigrant children whose parents typically have little education and/or do not speak English. Also an immigrant absorption policy that promotes investment in the official language skills after migration can enhance the value of the skills that immigrants bring with them.

Furthermore, our analysis also indicates that parental education, family size, and family income are important factors in school enrollment, which in turn implies that they play a strong role in educational attainment. Yet many black and Hispanic students are disadvantaged in this respect, signifying low rates of preschool and high school enrollment. Elementary and secondary schools can design alternative programs to help different groups overcome their socioeconomic disadvantage. Schools can try to intervene at different points in the education cycle by enacting special programs to reduce high school dropout rates and to increase enrollment rates. Since preschool prepares children for formal schooling, policies that encourage economically and socially disadvantaged families to enroll their children in preschool are also essential. Such policies will enable children from disadvantaged groups to start elementary school on an equal level with other children.

While immigration policy can control the quality of new immigrants, assimilation policies and educational reforms are still essential to ensure the quality of the future U.S. labor force. Given that currently, immigrants and children-of-immigrants constitute a large percentage of school age children, immigrant education needs to be a national policy that not only emphasizes that immigrant children enroll in school, but provides special programs such as ESL to help them overcome language barriers. It is essential to strengthen the school system that serves the immigrant communities so that the quality of schooling that immigrant children receive does not depend exclusively on the often inadequate resources of the local communities in which they reside—as is currently the case. In summary, the essential steps towards reducing the existing gap in educational attainment among different ethnic groups and countries-of-origin would be to institute programs that expedite English proficiency among adult immigrants, and educational reform to provide special educational programs to immigrant children to enable them to complete high school and go on to college.

APPENDIX

TABLE 29. DEFINITION OF VARIABLES

Variables	Code	Description
Dependent Variable:	Educational attainment	Highest level of education (20 categories)*.
	Enrollment	Dichotomous variable equal to unity if person enrolled in a public or private school, 0 otherwise.
Explanatory Variables:		
Gender variable	Male	Dichotomous variable equal to unity if gender is male and zero if gender is female.
Age variables	Age	Age in years.
	Age^2	Age squared.
	YSM	Years since migration*.
	YSM^2	Years since migration squared.
	Age-at-Immigration	Age-at-Immigration.
	Age-at-Immigration^2	Age-at-Immigration squared.
Race/Ethnicity	Black	Dichotomous variable equal to unity if race is black, 0 otherwise.
	Hispanic	Dichotomous variable equal to unity if race is Hispanic, 0 otherwise.
Birthplace	Foreign-Born	Dichotomous variable equal to unity if foreign-born, 0 otherwise; derived from Census/CPS variable on place of birth recode.
Region/Size of Place	South	Dichotomous variable equal to unity if person living in a South state, 0 otherwise.
	Rural	Dichotomous variable equal to unity if person living in a rural area, 0 otherwise.

TABLE 29 (continued)

Variables	Code	Description
Marital status	Married	Dichotomous variable equal to unity if married, spouse present, 0 otherwise.
Language variables	English Proficient	Dichotomous variable equal to unity if person speaks only English or speaks English very well, or speaks English well, 0 otherwise.
	LD	Linguistic Distance*.
Country-of-origin variables*	Africa	Dichotomous variable equal to unity if place of birth is Africa, 0 otherwise.
	Mexico	Dichotomous variable equal to unity if place of birth is Mexico, 0 otherwise.
	Cuba	Dichotomous variable equal to unity if place of birth is Cuba, 0 otherwise.
	S. & C. America	Dichotomous variable equal to unity if place of birth is South /Central America, 0 otherwise.
	Caribbean	Dichotomous variable equal to unity if place of birth is Caribbean, 0 otherwise.
	Southern Europe*	Dichotomous variable equal to unity if place of birth is Southern Europe, 0 otherwise.
	E. & C. Europe*	Dichotomous variable equal to unity if place of birth is East or Central Europe, 0 otherwise.
	N. & W. Europe*	Dichotomous variable equal to unity if place of birth is North or West Europe, 0 otherwise.
	Philippines	Dichotomous variable equal to unity if place of birth is Philippines, 0 otherwise.
	China	Dichotomous variable equal to unity if place of birth is China, 0 otherwise.
	Vietnam	Dichotomous variable equal to unity if place of birth is Vietnam, 0 otherwise.
	East Asia*	Dichotomous variable equal to unity if place of birth is East Asia, 0 otherwise.

TABLE 29 (continued)

Variables	Code	Description
	South Asia*	Dichotomous variable equal to unity if place of birth is South Asia, 0 otherwise.
	Middle East*	Dichotomous variable equal to unity if place of birth is Middle East, 0 otherwise.
	Other Asia*	Dichotomous variable equal to unity if place of birth is Other Asia, 0 otherwise.
	English-speaking countries*	Dichotomous variable equal to unity if place of birth is English-speaking countries, 0 otherwise.
	Remaining countries*	Dichotomous variable equal to unity if place of birth is remaining countries, 0 otherwise.
Age-at-immigration variables*	0 to 4	Dichotomous variable equal to unity if age-at-immigration between 0 and 4, 0 otherwise.
	5 to 12	Dichotomous variable equal to unity if age-at-immigration between 5 and 12, 0 otherwise.
	13 to 19	Dichotomous variable equal to unity if age-at-immigration between 13 and 19, 0 otherwise.
	20 to 24	Dichotomous variable equal to unity if age-at-immigration between 20 and 24, 0 otherwise.
	25 to 29	Dichotomous variable equal to unity if age-at-immigration between 25 and 29, 0 otherwise.
	30 to 34	Dichotomous variable equal to unity if age-at-immigration between 30 and 34, 0 otherwise.
	35 to 44	Dichotomous variable equal to unity if age-at-immigration between 35 and 44, 0 otherwise.
	45 to 64	Dichotomous variable equal to unity if age-at-immigration between 45 and 64, 0 otherwise.

TABLE 29 (continued)

Variables	Code	Description
Immigrant generation variables	First-generation	Dichotomous variable equal to unity if first-generation immigrant, 0 otherwise.
	Second-generation	Dichotomous variable equal to unity if second-generation immigrant, 0 otherwise.
	Mother foreign-born	Dichotomous variable equal to unity if second generation immigrant with foreign-born mother but non foreign-born father, 0 otherwise.
	Father foreign-born	Dichotomous variable equal to unity if second generation immigrant with foreign-born father but non foreign-born mother, 0 otherwise.
	Both parents foreign-born	Dichotomous variable equal to unity if second-generation immigrant with both parents foreign-born, 0 otherwise.
Family variables (for school enrollment only)	Household income	Annual household income received in 1989 in case of Census, and in 1995 in case of CPS.
	Net income	HHINC minus own earned income.
	0 Sibling	Dichotomous variable equal to unity if number of siblings is 0, 0 otherwise.
	1 Sibling	Dichotomous variable equal to unity if number of siblings is 1, 0 otherwise.
	2 Siblings	Dichotomous variable equal to unity if number of siblings is 2, 0 otherwise.
	3 Siblings	Dichotomous variable equal to unity if number of siblings is 3, 0 otherwise.
	4+ Siblings	Dichotomous variable equal to unity if number of siblings is greater than 4, 0 otherwise.
	Mother's education	Highest level of education attained by mother.
	Father's education	Highest level of education attained by father.

TABLE 29 (continued)

Variables	Code	Description
	Mother works full-time	Dichotomous variable equal to unity if mother works more than 35 hours per week, 0 otherwise.
	Mother works part-time	Dichotomous variable equal to unity if mother works less than 35 hours per week, 0 otherwise.
Age dummy variables (for school enrollment only)	Age3	Dichotomous variable equal to unity if age is 3 years, 0 otherwise.
	Age4	Dichotomous variable equal to unity if age is 4 years, 0 otherwise.
	Age5	Dichotomous variable equal to unity if age is 5 years, 0 otherwise.
	Age15	Dichotomous variable equal to unity if age is 15 years, 0 otherwise.
	Age16	Dichotomous variable equal to unity if age is 16 years, 0 otherwise.
	Age17	Dichotomous variable equal to unity if age is 17 years, 0 otherwise.
	Age18	Dichotomous variable equal to unity if age is 18 years, 0 otherwise.

*Additional information on Educational Attainment, YSM, Age-at-immigration, LD and Country-of-Origin variables.

Educational Attainment: The following categories were used for defining the number of years of schooling completed by the respondent: "no school completed or completed less than or equal to 4th grade" = 2.5 years; "completed between 5th and 8th grade" = 7 years; "completed 9th grade" = 9 years; "completed 10th grade" = 10 years; "completed 11th grade" = 11 years; "completed 12th grade with or without diploma, or completed GED" = 12 years; "some college, no degree, or associate degree" = 14 years; "Bachelors degree" = 16 years; "Masters degree" = 17.5 years; "Professional degree" = 18 years; "Doctorate degree" = 20 years.

YSM: The Census and CPS provide categorical information on year of immigration to the U.S. The Census calculations used 1990 as the base year while the CPS calculations used 1995 as the base year. The year of entry information is converted into a continuous measure (YSM) using the following values for the Census: "1987-1990" = 1.75 years; "1985-1986" = 4.25 years; "1982-1984" = 6.75 years; "1980-1981" = 9.25 years; "1975-1979" = 12.75 years; "1970-1974" = 17.75 years; "1965-1969" = 22.75 years; "1960-1964" = 27.75 years; "1950-1959" = 35.25 years; "Before 1950" = 49.75. For the CPS, the following values are used: "1992-1995" = 1.75 years; "1990-1991" = 4.25 years; "1988-1989" = 6.25 years; "1986-1987" = 8.25 years; "1984-1985" = 10.25 years; "1982-1983" = 12.25 years; "1980-1981" = 14.25 years; "1975-1979" = 17.75; "1970-1974" = 22.75: "1965-1969" = 27.75; "1960-1964" = 32.75; "1950-1959" = 40.25; "Before 1950" = 54.75.

Age-at-immigration: In order to create the age-at-immigration dummy variables, first a variable 'age-at-immigration (ageimmig)' is created. Ageimmig is calculated by subtracting YSM from current age. Thus ageimmig = YSM – Age. Since the Census and CPS provide the period on entry of immigrants into the U.S., YSM is calculated above. This approximation, however, results in some negative values when calculating 'ageimmig'. We encounter this problem of negative ageimmig values only for the two earliest periods (1950-59 and pre-1950) because compared to the other periods, the two early periods involve a much larger interval (10-year) approximated by the midpoint.

For example, a 34-year-old who migrated in 1957 (at the age of 1), has his YSM approximated as 35.5 and hence gets a -1.25 value for ageimmig. It is reasonable to assume that all the adults who get a negative calculated ageimmig probably immigrated at a very young age, therefore we assign them to the youngest age-at-immigration (0 to 4) group when we construct the age-at-immigration dummy variables.

LD: Linguistic distance is a measure of the difficulty of learning a foreign language for English-speaking Americans. It is based on a set of language scores, which measure achievements in speaking proficiency in foreign languages by English-speaking Americans. For the same number of weeks of instruction a lower language score (LS) represents lesser Language facility, and it is assumed, greater linguistic distance between English and the specific foreign language (Chiswick and Miller, 1998). Information on linguistic score for different language groups, and on the matching of these language groups to the 1990 Census-provided language codes, is obtained from English Language Fluency Among Immigrants in the United States, by B.R. Chiswick and P.W. Miller. People who reported speaking a language group for which we did not have a matching code were assigned mean scores (based on other members of the same birthplace group). Also foreign-born people who reported speaking English only at home (and therefore did not report a non-English language), were assigned the mean value of the linguistic scores for individuals from their birthplace group who reported a foreign language. The LS variable was constructed using the Census question, "What language, other than English is spoken at home?" The variable used in the regression equation is LD, which is a reciprocal of LS.

Country-of-Origin Variables: The country dummy variables marked with an asterix are discussed in further detail in this section. The remaining country dummy variables are self-explanatory.
Southern Europe includes Albania, Italy, Malta, Monaco, Portugal, Madeira Island, Spain, Vatican City, Yugoslavia.
East and Central Europe includes Austria, Belgium, Czechoslovakia, Denmark, Germany (East and West), Berlin (East and West), Liechtenstein, Luxembourg, Netherlands, Switzerland, Hungary, Poland, Romania, USSR, Baltic States, Estonia, Latvia, Lithuania.

North and West Europe includes Faroe Islands, Jan Mayen, Finland, Iceland, Norway, Sweden, Svalbard, Lapland, Andorra, France, Guernsey, Jersey, Azores Islands, Madeira Islands.

South Asia includes Afghanistan, Bangladesh, Bhutan, Burma, India, Pakistan, Sri Lanka, Nepal.

East Asia includes Japan, Korea, Macau, Mongolia, Taiwan.

Southeast Asia includes Brunei, Cambodia, Hong Kong, Indonesia, Laos, Malaysia, Singapore, Thailand, Indochina.

Middle East includes Bahrain, Cyprus, Iran, Iraq, Israel, Jordan, Kuwait, Lebanon, Qatar, Saudi Arabia, Syria, Turkey, United Arab Emirates, Yemen, Mesopotamia, Palestine, Persian Gulf States, West Bank.

English-speaking countries includes United Kingdom, England, Ireland, Scotland, Wales, Canada, Australia, New Zealand; English-speaking parts of Caribbean islands (Bahamas, British Virgin Islands, Jamaica, British West Indies).

Remaining includes all countries not included in the country dummy variables – the major composition being Oceania (except Australia and New Zealand).

TABLE 30. INDEX OF DIFFICULTY OF LEARNING A FOREIGN LANGUAGE (LANGUAGE SCORES)

Language	Direct Codes	Close Codes	Language Score
Africaana	611		3.00
Danish	615		2.25
Dutch	610	612	2.75
French	620	621,622,623,624	2.50
German	607	608,609,613	2.25
Italian	619		2.50
Norwegian	616	617,618	3.00
Portuguese	629	630	2.50
Rumanian	631	632	3.00
Spanish	625	626,627	2.25
Swedish	614		3.00
Indonesian	732	730-731,733-737	2.00
Malay	739		2.75
Swahili	791	792	2.75
Amharic	780		2.00
Bengali	664		1.75
Bulgarian	647	648	2.00
Burmese	717		1.75
Czech	642		2.00
Dari	660		2.00
Farsi	656	657,658,659,661	2.00
Finnish	679	680	2.00
Greek	637		1.75

TABLE 30 (continued)

Language	Direct Codes	Close Codes	Language Score
Hebrew	778		2.00
Hindi	663	662,665-669,678	1.75
Hungarian	682		2.00
Lao	720		1.50
Cambodian	726		2.00
Mongolian	694	695,716	2.00
Nepali	674		1.75
Polish	645	644,641	2.00
Russian	639	640,641	2.25
Serbo-Croatian	649-651	652	2.00
Sinhala	677		1.75
Tagalog	742	740,741,743-749	2.00
Thai	720	717,718,719	2.00
Turkish	691	689,690,692,693	2.00
Vietnamese	728	729	1.50
Arabic	777	779	1.50
Mandarin	712	713,714,715	1.50
Japanese	723	725	1.00
Korean	724		1.00
Cantonese	708	709,710,711,721,722	1.25

Source: Chiswick, B.R., and P.W. Miller. 1998. English Language Fluency among Immigrants in the United States. *Research in Labor Economics* 17: 151-200.

Note: Codes are from 1990 US Census of Population and Housing, Technical Documentation.

TABLE 31A. SCHOOL ENROLLMENT OF ADULTS BY AGE-AT-IMMIGRATION, UNITED STATES, 1990

Age-at-Immigration	Enrolled	Sample size
0 to 4	727 (12.67)[a]	5,738
5 to 12	1172 (11.71)	10,005
13 to 19	2351 (17.15)	19,861
20 to 24	3064 (12.65)	24,223
25 to 29	2657 (11.55)	23,006
30 to 34	1340 (10.03)	13,363
35 to 44	1033 (7.62)	13,565
45 to 64	374 (6.15)	6,078
Total	12,718 (10.97)	115,839

Source: 1990 Census of Population of United States, Public Use Microdata Sample, 1 percent file.

Note: Variables are as defined in Table 29 in Appendix.
[a] represents percent of specific age-at-immigration group sample enrolled (column 1 as a % of column 2 for each age-at-immigration group).

TABLE 31B. SCHOOL ENROLLMENT OF ADULTS BY AGE-AT-IMMIGRATION, UNITED STATES, 1995

Age-at-Immigration	Enrolled	Sample size
0 to 4	19 (6.29)[a]	302 (4.04)
5 to 12	41 (6.68)	614 (8.21)
13 to 19	65 (5.56)	1,170 (15.65)
20 to 24	107 (6.48)	1,652 (22.09)
25 to 29	107 (7.46)	1,435 (19.19)
30 to 34	43 (4.33)	992 (13.27)
35 to 44	35 (3.94)	889 (11.89)
45 to 64	8 (1.89)	424 (5.67)
Total	425 (5.68)	7,478

Source: October 1995 Current Population Survey, United States Census Bureau.

Note: Variables are as defined in Table 29 in Appendix A.
    [a] represents percent of specific age-at-immigration group sample enrolled (column 1 as a % of column 2 for each age-at-immigration group).

TABLE 32. REGRESSION ESTIMATES OF FOREIGN-BORN ADULTS BY HISPANIC/NON-HISPANIC ORIGIN, UNITED STATES, 1990

DEPENDENT VARIABLE: EDUCATIONAL ATTAINMENT

Variable	Hispanic		Non-Hispanic	
	(1)	(2)	(1)	(2)
Constant	11.013	9.308	10.803	10.335
	(34.63)	(27.55)	(47.64)	(44.11)
Male	-0.087	-0.081	0.902	0.883
	(2.15)	(2.00)	(32.59)	(31.84)
Age	0.081	0.027	0.177	0.178
	(4.98)	(1.66)	(16.31)	(15.99)
Age^2	-0.001	-0.060	-0.003	-0.003
	(6.01)	(3.14)	(21.01)	(20.59)
Black	1.309	1.275	-0.729	-0.601
	(10.66)	(10.42)	(14.08)	(12.21)
Married	-0.123	-0.090	-0.010	-0.024
	(2.75)	(2.01)	(0.31)	(0.73)
South	0.700	0.664	0.449	0.465
	(15.85)	(15.07)	(12.84)	(13.30)
Rural	-1.941	-1.1905	-0.224	-0.169
	(24.79)	(24.43)	(4.50)	(3.42)
Age-at-immigration (Ageimmig)	-0.174	n.e.	0.011	n.e.
	(26.61)		(2.90)	
$Ageimmig^2/100$	0.198	n.e.	-0.08	n.e.
	(15.86)		(10.62)	
LD * Non-English	n.e.	n.e.	0.610	n.e.
			(7.10)	
Non-English	n.e.	n.e.	-0.865	n.e.
			(14.43)	
AGE-AT-IMMIGRATION				
0 to 4	n.e.	2.746	n.e.	0.289
		(24.41)		(4.35)
5 to 12	n.e.	2.101	n.e.	0.112
		(24.60)		(2.02)
13 to 19	n.e.	-0.129	n.e.	-0.336
		(1.95)		(7.09)
20 to 24	n.e.	-0.157	n.e.	-0.170
		(2.41)		(3.95)
30 to 34	n.e.	-0.230	n.e.	-0.330
		(2.92)		(6.58)
35 to 44	n.e.	-0.660	n.e.	-0.77
		(8.08)		(15.21)
45 to 64	n.e.	-1.166	n.e.	-1.394
		(9.86)		(20.34)
Adjusted R^2	0.061	0.067	0.70	0.068
Sample size	46,010	46,010	69,829	69,829

Source: 1990 Census of Population of United States, Public Use Microdata Sample, 1 percent file.

Note: Variables are as defined in Table 29 in Appendix.

n.e. = Variable not entered. t statistics are in parentheses.

TABLE 33. REGRESSION ESTIMATES OF FIRST-GENERATION ADULTS BY HISPANIC/NON-HISPANIC ORIGIN, UNITED STATES, 1995

DEPENDENT VARIABLE: EDUCATIONAL ATTAINMENT

Variable	Hispanic		Non-Hispanic	
	(1)	(2)	(1)	(2)
Constant	11.807	9/678	11.821	12.176
	(10.03)	(7.84)	(14.21)	(13.85)
Male	0.020	0.056	0.756	0.755
	(0.13)	(0.38)	(7.46)	(7.45)
Age	0.066	0.016	0.122	0.113
	(1.12)	(0.27)	(3.03)	(2.69)
Age^2	-0.079	-0.030	-0.002	-0.002
	(1.13)	(0.42)	(4.24)	(3.84)
Black	2.516	2.432	-0.821	-0.796
	(5.50)	(5.33)	(4.80)	(4.66)
Married	-0.274	-0.256	0.261	0.246
	(1.70)	(1.59)	(2.20)	(2.07)
South	0.280	0.224	0.331	0.317
	(1.63)	(1.31)	(2.38)	(2.27)
Non-MSA	-1.197	-1.221	-0.257	-0.235
	(4.20)	(4.30)	(1.18)	(1.08)
Age-at-immigration (Ageimmig)	-0.184	n.e.	0.009	n.e.
	(7.27)		(0.59)	
Ageimmig^2/100	0.002	n.e.	-0.056	n.e.
	(4.06)		(2.15)	
AGE-AT-IMMIGRATION				
0 to 4	n.e.	3.092	n.e.	0.148
		(6.96)		(0.56)
5 to 12	n.e.	2.402	n.e.	-0.103
		(7.84)		(0.49)
13 to 19	n.e.	0.133	n.e.	-0.641
		(0.56)		(3.46)
20 to 24	n.e.	-0.013	n.e.	-0.368
		(0.06)		(2.31)
30 to 34	n.e.	-0.243	n.e.	0.352
		(0.89)		(1.97)
35 to 44	n.e.	-0.469	n.e.	0.782
		(1.49)		(4.24)
45 to 64	n.e.	-1.509	n.e.	-1.338
		(3.34)		(5.46)
Adjusted R^2	0.061	0.068	0.057	0.061
Sample size	2,858	2,858	4,638	4,638

Source: October 1995 Current Population Survey, United States Census Bureau.

Note: Variables are as defined in Table 29 in Appendix.

n.e. = Variable not entered. t statistics are in parentheses.

TABLE 34. MARGINAL EFFECTS OF POOLED SAMPLE OF FIRST-GENERATION, SECOND-GENERATION, AND NATIVE-PARENTAGE CHILDREN, UNITED STATES, 1990

DEPENDENT VARIABLE: SCHOOL ENROLLMENT

AGE GROUP 3 TO 5 YEARS

Variable	(1)	(2)[a]
Male	0.001	0.001
Age3	-0.235	-0.236
Age5	0.301	0.301
Black	0.069	0.070
Hispanic	0.001	0.003
South	0.006	0.005
Rural	-0.083	-0.082
English proficiency	-0.058	-0.060
Mother's education	0.019	0.019
Father's education	0.011	0.011
Mother works full-time	0.014	0.014
Mother works part-time	0.061	0.061
1 Sibling	0.467	0.018
2 Sibling	0.011	0.011
3 Sibling	-0.021	-0.022
4+ Sibling	-0.031	-0.032
Household income	2.12e-06	2.11e-06
First-generation	0.096	n.e.
Second-generation	0.038	0.038

TABLE 34 (continued)

Variable	(1)	(2)[a]
Age-at-immigration 2+	-0.062	-0.053
BIRTHPLACE		
English-speaking countries	n.e.	0.191
Africa	n.e.	0.035
Mexico	n.e.	0.084
Cuba	n.e.	0.425
S. & C. America	n.e.	0.063
Caribbean	n.e.	-0.125
Southern Europe	n.e.	0.138
E. & C. Europe	n.e.	-0.023
N. & W. Europe	n.e.	0.425
Philippines	n.e.	0.058
China	n.e.	0.241
Vietnam	n.e.	0.175
East Asia	n.e.	0.102
South Asia	n.e.	0.021
Middle East	n.e.	-0.057
Other Asia	n.e.	0.178
Remaining countries	n.e.	0.218
Pseudo R^2	0.174	0.174
Sample size	80,714	80,714

Source: Table 14, Chapter 6

Note: Variables are as defined in Table 29 in Appendix.
   n.e. = Variable not entered.
   [a] benchmark group is all 3- to 5-year age group native-parentage children.

TABLE 35. MARGINAL EFFECTS OF FIRST-GENERATION CHILDREN, UNITED STATES, 1990

DEPENDENT VARIABLE: SCHOOL ENROLLMENT

AGE GROUP 3 TO 5 YEARS

Variable	(1)	(2)[a]
Male	0.023	0.020
Age3	-0.238	-0.254
Age5	0.341	0.345
Black	-0.006	0.010
Hispanic	-0.064	0.022
South	0.037	0.019
Rural	0.003	-0.001
English proficiency	0.027	0.026
Mother's education	0.010	0.010
Father's education	0.009	0.009
Mother works full-time	0.011	0.009
Mother works part-time	0.081	0.071
1 Sibling	0.107	0.122
2 Sibling	0.036	0.040
3 Sibling	0.035	0.058
4+ Siblings	0.133	0.166
Household income	1.74e-06	1.40e-06
Age-at-immigration 2+	-0.064	-0.068

TABLE 35 (continued)

Variable	(1)	(2)[a]
BIRTHPLACE		
Africa	n.e.	-0.116
Mexico	n.e.	-0.223
Cuba	n.e.	0.303
S. & C. America	n.e.	-0.156
Caribbean	n.e.	-0.271
Southern Europe	n.e.	-0.088
E. & C. Europe	n.e.	-0.191
N. & W. Europe	n.e.	0.294
Philippines	n.e.	0.141
China	n.e.	0.072
Vietnam	n.e.	-0.121
East Asia	n.e.	-0.052
South Asia	n.e.	-0.168
Middle East	n.e.	-0.231
Other Asia	n.e.	-0.124
Remaining countries	n.e.	-0.036
Pseudo R^2	0.182	0.200
Sample size	1,556	1,556

Source: Table 16, Chapter 6.

Note: Variables are as defined in Table 29 in Appendix.
n.e. = Variable not entered.
[a] benchmark group is all 3- to 5-year age group native-parentage children.

TABLE 36. MARGINAL EFFECTS OF SECOND-GENERATION AND NATIVE-PARENTAGE CHILDREN, UNITED STATES, 1990

DEPENDENT VARIABLE: SCHOOL ENROLLMENT

AGE GROUP 3 TO 5 YEARS

Variable	Second-Generation	Native-Parentage	All Native-Born
Male	0.002	-0.001	0.001
Age3	-0.253	-0.234	-0.236
Age5	0.333	0.299	0.301
Black	0.078	0.076	0.071
Hispanic	-0.043	-0.005	0.003
South	0.035	0.002	0.006
Rural	-0.059	-0.079	-0.082
English proficiency	-0.010	-0.054	-0.068
Mother's education	0.011	0.024	0.020
Father's education	0.004	0.015	0.012
Mother works full-time	0.006	0.015	0.013
Mother works part-time	0.046	0.060	0.061
1 Sibling	0.022	0.013	0.016
2 Sibling	0.045	0.004	0.010
3 Sibling	0.007	-0.030	-0.023
4+ Siblings	0.013	-0.059	-0.041
Household income	1.98e-06	2.03e-06	2.10e-06
Mother foreign-born	n.e.	n.e.	0.020
Father foreign-born	n.e.	n.e.	0.030
Both parents foreign-born	n.e.	n.e.	0.051
Pseudo R^2	0.197	0.173	0.174
Sample size	9,392	69,766	79,158

Source: Table 17, Chapter 6.

Note: Variables are as defined in Table 29 in Appendix.
    n.e. = Variable not entered.

TABLE 37. MARGINAL EFFECTS OF POOLED SAMPLE OF FIRST-GENERATION, SECOND-GENERATION, AND NATIVE-PARENTAGE CHILDREN, UNITED STATES, 1995

DEPENDENT VARIABLE: SCHOOL ENROLLMENT

AGE GROUP 3 TO 5 YEARS

Variable	(1)
Male	-0.079
Age3	-0.691
Age5	1.359
Black	0.020
Hispanic	0.056
South	0.015
Non-MSA	-0.196
First-generation	0.453
Second-generation	-0.123
Age-at-immigration 2+	-0.217
Household income	7.25e-06
Mother's education	0.052
Father's education	0.031
Mother works full-time	0.032
Mother works part-time	0.206
Pseudo R^2	0.262
Sample size	4,327

Source: Table 28, Chapter 6.

Note: Variables are as defined in Table 29 in Appendix.

TABLE 38. MARGINAL EFFECTS OF SECOND-GENERATION AND NATIVE-PARENTAGE CHILDREN, UNITED STATES, 1995

DEPENDENT VARIABLE: SCHOOL ENROLLMENT

AGE GROUP 3 TO 5 YEARS

Variable	Second-Generation	Native-Parentage	All Native-Born
Male	-0.069	-0.023	-0.028
Age3	-0.358	-0.223	-0.245
Age5	0.459	0.370	0.384
Black	0.106	-0.012	0.002
Hispanic	-0.083	0.041	0.010
South	-0.058	0.015	0.004
Non-MSA	-0.072	-0.059	-0.068
Household income	7.87e-07	2.55e-06	2.42e-06
Mother's education	0.008	0.023	0.018
Father's education	0.015	0.009	0.011
Mother works full-time	0.009	0.008	0.011
Mother works part-time	0.073	0.066	0.067
Mother foreign-born	n.e.	n.e.	-0.064
Father foreign-born	n.e.	n.e.	-0.034
Both parents foreign-born	n.e.	n.e.	-0.034
Pseudo R^2	0.317	0.250	0.260
Sample size	708	3,541	4,249

Source: Table 20, Chapter 6.

Note: Variables are as defined in Table 29 in Appendix.
  n.e. = Variable not entered.

TABLE 39. MARGINAL EFFECTS OF POOLED SAMPLE OF FIRST-GENERATION, SECOND-GENERATION, AND NATIVE-PARENTAGE CHILDREN, UNITED STATES, 1990

DEPENDENT VARIABLE: SCHOOL ENROLLMENT

AGE GROUP 16 TO 18 YEARS

Variable	(1)	(2)[a]
Male	-0.010	-0.010
Age17	-0.033	-0.033
Age18	-0.156	-0.156
Black	0.008	0.008
Hispanic	0.005	0.010
South	-0.005	-0.005
Rural	0.008	0.009
English proficiency	0.069	0.073
Mother's education	0.007	0.007
Father's education	0.007	0.007
Mother works full-time	0.006	0.006
Mother works part-time	0.014	0.014
1 Sibling	0.019	0.019
2 Sibling	0.011	0.010
3 Sibling	0.004	0.004
4+ Sibling	-0.014	-0.14
Household income	2.94e-07	2.98e-07
First-generation	0.048	n.e.
Second-generation	0.038	0.036
Age-at-immigration 5 to 12	0.015	0.008
Age-at-immigration 13 to 18	-0.029	-0.037

TABLE 39 (continued)

Variable	(1)	(2)[a]
BIRTHPLACE		
English-speaking countries	n.e.	0.038
Africa	n.e.	0.038
Mexico	n.e.	0.042
Cuba	n.e.	0.035
S. & C. America	n.e.	0.043
Caribbean	n.e.	0.075
Southern Europe	n.e.	0.044
E. & C. Europe	n.e.	0.036
N. & W. Europe	n.e.	-0.010
Philippines	n.e.	0.018
China	n.e.	0.065
Vietnam	n.e.	0.066
East Asia	n.e.	0.059
South Asia	n.e.	0.074
Middle East	n.e.	0.047
Other Asia	n.e.	0.071
Remaining countries	n.e.	0.020
Pseudo R^2	0.111	0.112
Sample size	65,718	65,718

Source: Table 22, Chapter 7.

Note: Variables are as defined in Table 29 in Appendix.
   n.e. = Variable not entered.
   [a] benchmark group is all 16- to 18- year age group native-parentage children.

TABLE 40. MARGINAL EFFECTS OF FIRST-GENERATION CHILDREN, UNITED STATES, 1990

DEPENDENT VARIABLE: SCHOOL ENROLLMENT

AGE GROUP 16 TO 18 YEARS

Variable	(1)	(2)[a]
Male	-0.112	-0.016
Age17	-0.280	-0.045
Age18	-0.545	-0.089
Black	-0.022	-0.013
Hispanic	-0.334	-0.023
South	0.168	0.022
Rural	-0.318	-0.049
English proficiency	0.842	0.192
Mother's education	0.014	0.002
Father's education	0.022	0.002
Mother works full-time	0.025	0.005
Mother works part-time	-0.166	-0.024
1 Sibling	0.204	0.027
2 Sibling	0.115	0.015
3 Sibling	0.220	0.028
4+ Siblings	0.077	0.014
Household income	1.14e-06	2.07e-06
Age-at-immigration 5 to 12	0.018	-0.004
Age-at-immigration 13 to 18	-0.044	-0.014

TABLE 40 (continued)

Variable	(1)	(2)[a]
BIRTHPLACE		
Africa	n.e.	-0.001
Mexico	n.e.	-0.018
Cuba	n.e.	-0.017
S. & C. America	n.e.	0.011
Caribbean	n.e.	0.069
Southern Europe	n.e.	-0.017
E. & C. Europe	n.e.	0.009
N. & W. Europe	n.e.	-0.108
Philippines	n.e.	-0.018
China	n.e.	0.035
Vietnam	n.e.	0.033
East Asia	n.e.	0.038
South Asia	n.e.	0.067
Middle East	n.e.	-0.003
Other Asia	n.e.	0.033
Remaining countries	n.e.	-0.035
Pseudo R^2	0.140	0.156
Sample size	3,560	3,560

Source: Table 24, Chapter 7.

Note: Variables are as defined in Table 29 in Appendix.
n.e. = Variable not entered.
[a] benchmark group is all first-generation 16- to 18-year age group children from English-speaking countries.

TABLE 41. MARGINAL EFFECTS OF SECOND-GENERATION AND NATIVE-PARENTAGE CHILDREN, UNITED STATES, 1990

DEPENDENT VARIABLE: SCHOOL ENROLLMENT

AGE GROUP 16 TO 18 YEARS

Variable	Second-Generation	Native-Parentage	All Native-Born
Male	0.002	-0.010	-0.009
Age17	-0.042	-0.031	-0.032
Age18	-0.126	-0.163	-0.160
Black	-0.023	0.013	0.010
Hispanic	0.001	0.003	0.010
South	0.004	-0.006	-0.005
Rural	-0.023	0.014	0.011
English proficiency	0.037	-0.002	0.010
Mother's education	0.003	0.010	0.009
Father's education	0.004	0.008	0.007
Mother works full-time	0.002	0.004	0.005
Mother works part-time	0.001	0.015	0.015
1 Sibling	0.003	0.019	0.018
2 Sibling	0.009	0.010	0.010
3 Sibling	-0.010	0.001	0.001
4+ Siblings	-0.009	-0.023	-0.020
Household income	1.67e-07	2.65e-07	2.66e-06
Mother foreign-born	n.e.	n.e.	0.024
Father foreign-born	n.e.	n.e.	0.015
Both parents foreign-born	n.e.	n.e.	0.053
Pseudo R^2	0.075	0.121	0.115
Sample size	5,401	56,757	62,158

Source: Table 25, Chapter 7.

Note: Variables are as defined in Table 29 in Appendix A.
    n.e. = Variable not entered.

TABLE 42. MARGINAL EFFECTS OF POOLED SAMPLE OF FIRST-GENERATION, SECOND-GENERATION, AND NATIVE-PARENTAGE CHILDREN, UNITED STATES, 1995

DEPENDENT VARIABLE: SCHOOL ENROLLMENT

AGE GROUP 15 TO 18 YEARS

Variable	(1)
Male	-0.008
Age15	0.025
Age17	-0.16
Age18	-0.175
Black	0.017
Hispanic	-0.004
South	-0.004
Non-MSA	0.012
First-generation	0.019
Second-generation	0.026
Age-at-immigration 5 to 12	0.008
Age-at-immigration 13 to 18	-0.016
Household income	4.30e-07
Mother's education	0.004
Father's education	0.003
Mother works full-time	0.014
Mother works part-time	0.013
Pseudo R^2	0.267
Sample size	4,949

Source: Table 27, Chapter 7.

Note: Variables are as defined in Table 29 in Appendix.

**TABLE 43. MARGINAL EFFECTS OF SECOND-GENERATION AND
NATIVE-PARENTAGE CHILDREN, UNITED STATES, 1995**

DEPENDENT VARIABLE: SCHOOL ENROLLMENT

AGE GROUP 15 TO 18 YEARS

Variable	Second-Generation	Native-Parentage	All Native-Born
Male	0.010	-0.007	0.005
Age15	dropped	0.021	0.023
Age17	0.011	-0.018	-0.014
Age18	-0.135	-0.188	-0.170
Black	dropped	0.015	0.015
Hispanic	-0.044	-0.001	-0.003
South	-0.008	-0.001	-0.002
Non-MSA	dropped	0.013	0.013
Household income	3.85e-07	3.94e-07	3.79e-06
Mother's education	-0.003	0.007	0.005
Father's education	0.007	0.004	0.004
Mother works full-time	-0.006	0.014	0.012
Mother works part-time	-0.008	0.012	0.011
Mother foreign-born	n.e.	n.e.	0.023
Father foreign-born	n.e.	n.e.	0.012
Both parents foreign-born	n.e.	n.e.	0.026
Pseudo R^2	0.223	0.295	0.280
Sample size	310	4,161	4,693

Source: Table 28, Chapter 7.

Note: Variables are as defined in Table 29 in Appendix.
n.e. = Variable not entered.

NOTES

1. Notable exceptions for the U.S. include White and Glick (2000) and Glick and White (2003a, 2003b) and Chiswick and DebBurman (2004).

2. Studies in the sociological literature often use a socioeconomic status score or index rather than separate variables for parental education and income. They find very strong effects of socioeconomic status on children's schooling performance and attainment from kindergarten to post-secondary school education. See for example, Glick and White (2003a, 2003b), White and Glick (2000), and Tach and Farkas (2003).

3. Other studies also find a negative effect of the number of siblings on a child's educational attainment. See, for example, Glick and White (2003a).

4. For recent assessments of the ongoing debate, see Bowles and Gintis (2002) and Farkas (2003).

5. There are two costs associated with post-migration investment in schooling - the direct cost of college expense in the United States, and the indirect foregone earnings in the country-of-origin. Testing the effect of age on post-migration education provides an indirect measure of the opportunity cost of foregone earnings, and this approach is used in our study.

6. Total schooling acquired may be affected by pre-immigration schooling in two ways. One is the quantity measure of pre-immigration schooling, which is years of schooling completed in the origin. Two, holding quantity constant, the quality of pre-immigration schooling may differ by country-of-origin. For example, the knowledge acquired through ten years of schooling in Mexico could be quite different from the same number of years of schooling in Sweden. In general, education systems in some countries are known to be more rigorous than others. While the importance of quality of pre-immigration schooling cannot be denied, it is difficult to obtain data measures of schooling by country-of-origin that would account for such differences, therefore, it is beyond the scope of this work to investigate the qualitative effects of pre-immigration schooling on total schooling, other than through dichotomous country-of-origin (fixed effects) variables.

7. Another variable that reflects post-migration investment in schooling is the current enrollment status of the immigrant. While the importance of analyzing current enrollment status in a study of educational attainment is recognized, it is beyond the scope of this work to conduct an in-depth analysis of enrollment status among adult immigrants. However, to get a picture of how enrollment

rates may vary by age-at-immigration, a frequency distribution of current enrollment status by age-at-immigration is reported in Table 31, Parts A and B.

8. The nature of the data used for this study makes it difficult to conduct the enrollment analysis for children above 18 years who typically live away from home. However, with growing importance placed on post-secondary education, an analysis of college enrollment rates and other aspects of post-secondary education by immigrant groups warrants further research.

9. Data constraints prevent us from analyzing the enrollment pattern of children from single-parent homes. This exclusion has certain implications because a large portion of school age children increasingly come from single-parent households. It should be noted that results that hold true for the two-parent household might not fully explain the enrollment behavior of children from single-parent households.

10. The age variable captures two effects: one, the cohort effect (younger cohorts acquire more education) and two, the life cycle effect (education increases with age in the life cycle). Due to the secular increase in schooling, beyond a certain point the negative cohort effect of an older age dominates the positive life cycle effect.

11. See section on Educational Attainment of Foreign-born adults for a more detailed discussion on this issue

12. If Education = ...+ b_1(Foreign-born) + b_2(Ageimmig)*(Foreign-born) + b_3 (Ageimmig)^2 *(Foreign-born), then taking derivatives

δ (Education)/δ(Foreign-born) = b_1 + b_2 (Ageimmig) + b_3 (Ageimmig)^2

13. If Education = ...+ b_1 (LD*Non-english) + b_2 (Non-english), then taking derivatives

δ (Education)/δ (LD) = b_1 + b_2 for Non-english = 1
    = 0 for Non-english = 0

14. Specification 3 is also run with the LD variable included. The significance and magnitude of the LD variable falls from 0.96 to 0.03 with the introduction of the country dummy variables, but the country coefficients remain more or less unchanged. The change in the partial effect of LD is quite pronounced but this change is not surprising given the close co-relation between birthplace and LD. It is reasonable to assume that the birthplace dummy variables account for most of the variation in the LD coefficient.

15. Education = ...+ b_1 (LD*non-English) + b_2 (non-English)

δ (Education)/δ (LD) = (1.001) + (-0.969) for Non-english = 1
    = 0 for Non-english = 0

16. Specification 3 is also run with the LD variable. When running this specification on the foreign-born sample, the dummy for English-speaking country negates the need for a separate non-English dummy. The country dummy variables have a pronounced effect on LD, which turns from 0.03 to − 0.74. We expect the LD variable to be closely related to the country-of-origin dummy variables, hence the country coefficients capture a major portion of the LD effect.

17. The summary statistics discussed in Table 7 indicated a large proportion of the first-generation sample to be Hispanic. To test if the Hispanic pool dominates the results derived from our analysis of the foreign-born sample, the basic specification (only demographic and geographic variables) and the specification with age-at-immigration dummy variables were run separately on the Hispanic sample and the non-Hispanic sample (see Table 32 and 33, Appendix).

18. Since a majority of the country-of-origin dummies were insignificant, the predicted probabilities were re-calculated on a modified version of specification 2 which included only the significant variables. Omission of the insignificant variables had minimal/no effect on the original predicted probabilities.

19. To test if the sign of Hispanic was sensitive to the sample sizes of the three major Hispanic source countries, Mexico, Cuba, and South and Central America, the three countries-of-origin, Mexico, Cuba, South and Central America, were combined into a single country dummy and specification 2 was re-run. The combined country dummy was statistically insignificant and Hispanic continued to be insignificant.

20. Since a majority of the country-of-origin dummies are insignificant, the predicted probabilities were re-calculated on a modified version of specification 2 which included only the significant variables. Omission of the insignificant variables raised the predicted probabilities associated with Mexico, the Caribbean, and the Middle East, but lowered the probability associated with South Asia.

21. See Barnett, S.W. (1992): Benefits of Compensatory Preschool Education. Journal of Human Resources. 27 (1); 279-312.

22. To test if the sign of Hispanic was sensitive to the sample sizes of the three major Hispanic source countries, Mexico, Cuba, and South and Central America, the three countries-of-origin, Mexico, Cuba, South and Central America, were combined into a single country dummy and specification 2 was re-run. The combined country dummy was statistically insignificant and Hispanic continued to be insignificant.

23. Since a majority of the country-of-origin dummies were insignificant, the predicted probabilities were re-calculated on a modified version of specification 2 which included only the significant variables. Omission of the insignificant variables raised the predicted probability of the reference group to 0.95 and the probabilities of the Caribbean and South Asia to 0.99.

REFERENCES

Arias, B. 1986. The context of education for Hispanic students: An overview. *American Journal of Education* 95: 26-57.

Becker, G.S. 1964. *Human capital: A theoretical and empirical analysis, with special reference to education.* 2nd ed. New York: National Bureau of Economic Research, Columbia University Press.

Becker, G.S. 1967. *Human capital and the personal distribution of income.* Wyotinsky Lecture, No. 1. Ann Arbor: University of Michigan.

Becker, G.S. 1993. *Human capital: A theoretical and empirical analysis, with special reference to education.* 3rd ed. Chicago: University of Chicago Press.

Becker, G.S., and H.G. Lewis. 1973. On the interaction between the quantity and quality of children. *Journal of Political Economy* 81(2): S279-S288.

Becker, G.S., and N. Tomes. 1976. Child endowments and the quantity and quality of children. *Journal of Political Economy* 84 (4): S143-S162.

Behrman, J.R., R. Pollak, and P. Taubman. 1995. *From parent to child: Intrahousehold allocations and intergenerational relations in the United States.* Chicago: University of Chicago Press.

Berk, L. 1985. Relationship of educational attainment, child oriented attitudes, job satisfaction, and career commitment to caregiver behavior toward children. *Child Care Quarterly* 14: 103-129.

Betts, J.R., and M. Lofstrom. 2000. The educational attainment of immigrants: Trends and implications. In *Issues in the Economics of Immigration*, edited by G.J. Borjas, 51-117. University of Chicago Press.

Blau, D.M., and P.K. Robins. 1988. Child-care costs and family labor supply. *The Review of Economics and Statistics* 52 (3): 374-81.

Borjas, G.J. 1982. The earnings of male Hispanic immigrants in the United States. *Industrial and Labor Relations Review* 35 (3): 343-353.

Borjas, G.J. 1987. Self-selection and the earnings of immigrants. *American Economic Review* 77 (4): 531-553.

Borjas, G.J. 1992. Ethnic capital and intergenerational mobility. *Quarterly Journal of Economics* 107 (1): 123-150.

Bowles, S., and H. Gintis. 2002. Schooling in capitalistic America revisited. *Sociology of Education* 75: 1-18.

Brayfield, A., and S.L. Hofferth. 1995. Balancing the family budget: Differences in child care expenditures by race/ethnicity, economic status, and family structure. *Social Science Quarterly* 76 (1): 158-77.

Cardak, B., and J.T. McDonald. 2004. Neighborhood effects, preference heterogeneity and immigrant educational attainment. *Applied Economics* 36 (6): 559-72.

Carter, T.P., and D.R. Segura. 1979. *Mexican Americans in School: A Decade of Change.* New York: College Entrance Examination Board.

Chiswick, B.R. 1977. Sons of immigrants: Are they at an earnings disadvantage? *American Economic Association, Papers and Proceedings.* 376-380.

Chiswick, B.R. 1978a. The effect of Americanization on the earnings of foreign-born men. *Journal of Political Economy* 86 (5): 897-922.

Chiswick, B.R. 1978b. Generating inequality: absolute or relative schooling inequality? *Journal of Human Resources* 13 (1): 135-37.

Chiswick, B.R. 1979. The economic progress of immigrants: Some apparently universal patterns. In *Contemporary Economic Problems,* edited by W. Fellner, 359-399. Washington, D.C.: American Enterprise Institute for Public Policy Research.

Chiswick, B.R. 1986. Labor supply and investments in child quality: A study of Jewish and non-Jewish women. *Review of Economics and Statistics* 68 (4): 700-703.

Chiswick, B.R. 1988. Differences in education and earnings across racial and ethnic groups: Tastes, discrimination, and investments in child quality. *Quarterly Journal of Economics* 103 (3): 571-97.

Chiswick, B.R. 1991. Speaking, reading, and earnings among low-skilled immigrants. *Journal of Labor Economics* 9 (2): 149-170.

Chiswick, B.R. 1999. Are immigrants favorably self-selected? *American Economic Review* 89 (2): 181-185.

Chiswick, B.R., and N. DebBurman. 2004. Educational attainment: Analysis by immigrant generation. *Economics of Education Review* 23: 361-379.

Chiswick, B.R., and P.W. Miller. 1992. Immigration, language, and ethnicity: Canada and the United States. In *Language in the Immigrant Labor Market,* edited by B.R. Chiswick, 229-96. Washington, D.C., AEI Press.

Chiswick, B.R., and P.W. Miller. 1994. The determinants of post-immigration investments in education. *Economics of Education Review* 13 (2): 163-177.

Chiswick, B.R., and P.W. Miller. 1995. The endogeny between language and earnings: International analysis. *Journal of Labor Economics* 13 (2): 246-88.

Chiswick, B.R., and P.W. Miller. 1998. English language fluency among immigrants in the United States. *Research in Labor Economics* 17: 151-200.

Chiswick, B.R., and P.W. Miller. 1999. Language skills and earnings among legalized aliens. *Journal of Population Economics* 12 (1): 63-89.

Chiswick, B.R., and P.W. Miller. 2001. A model of destination language acquisition: Application to male immigrants in Canada. *Demography* 38(3): 391-409.

Chiswick, B.R., and P.W. Miller. 2003. The complementarity of language and other human capital: Immigrant earnings in Canada. *Economics of Education Review* 22(5): 469-80.

Chiswick, B.R, and T.A. Sullivan. 1995. The new immigrants. In *State of the Union: America in the 1990's*, edited by Reynolds Farley, 211-270. New York: Russell Sage Foundation.

Cobb-Clark, D., M.D. Connolly, and C. Worswick. 2004. Post-migration investments in job search and education: A family perspective. *Journal of Population Economics* (forthcoming).

Cohen, Y., T. Zach, and B.R. Chiswick. 1997. The educational attainment of immigrants: Changes over time. *Quarterly Review of Economics and Finance* 37 (Special Issue 1997): 229-243.

Connelly, R., and J. Kimmel. 2003. Marital status and full-time/part-time work status in child care choices. *Applied Economics* 35 (7): 761-77.

Datcher-Loury, L. 1988. Effects of mother's home time on children's schooling. *Review of Economics and Statistics* 70 (3): 367-73.

Dicks, G., and A. Sweetman. 1999. Education and ethnicity in Canada: An intergenerational perspective. *Journal of Human Resources* 34 (4): 668-96.

Djajic, S. 2003. Assimilation of immigrants: Implications for human capital accumulation of the second generation. *Journal of Population Economics* 16(4): 831-45.

Duleep, H., and M.C. Regets. 1999. Immigrants and human-capital investment. *American Economic Review* 89 (2): 186-191.

Duncan, G.J. 1994. Families and neighbors as sources of disadvantage in the schooling decisions of white and black adolescents. *American Journal of Education* 103 (1): 20-53.

Duncan, G.J., and C.R. Hill. 1977. The child care mode choices of working mothers. In *Patterns of Economic Progress, Vol. 5*, edited by G. Duncan and J.N. Morgan, 379-388. Ann Arbor: Institute for Social Research.

Dustmann, C.1994. Speaking fluency, writing fluency and earnings of migrants in Germany. *Journal of Population Economics* 7 (2): 133-156.

Dustmann, C. 1997. The effects of education, parental background and ethnic concentration on language. *Quarterly Review of Economics and Finance* 37 (Special Issue 1997): 245-262.

Dustmann, C. 2003. Language proficiency and labor market performance of immigrants in the U.K. *Economic Journal* 113 (489): 695-717.

Edwards, L.N. 1975. The economics of schooling decisions: Teenage enrollment rates. *Journal of Human Resources* 10 (2): 155-73.

Ellis, R. 1994. *The Study of Second Language Acquisition*, 327-329. Oxford University Press.

Evans, M.D.R. 1986. Sources of immigrant's language proficiency. Australian results with comparisons to the Federal Republic of Germany and the United States of America. *European Sociological Review* 2: 226-236.

Fan, C.S. 1997. The value of time and the interaction of the quantity and the quality of children. *Seoul Journal of Economics* 10 (2): 135-58.

Farkas, G. 2003. Cognitive skills and noncognitive traits and behaviours in stratification processes. *Annual Review of Sociology* 29: 541-62.

Francis, P., and P. Self. 1982. Initiative responsiveness of young children in day care and home settings: The importance of the child to caregiver ratio. *Child Study Journal* 12 (1): 119-126.

Friedberg, R. 1993. *The Labor Market Assimilation of Immigrants in the U.S.: The Role of Age at Arrival.* Providence, R.I.: Brown University.

Funkhouser, E. 1995. How much of immigrant wage assimilation is related to English language acquisition. *University of California, Santa Barbara, Working Papers in Economics*: 01/96.

Funkhouser, E., and S.J. Trejo. 1995. The labor market skills of recent immigrants: Evidence from the CPS. *Industrial and Labor Relations Review* 48 (4): 792-811.

Gang, I.N. 1997. Schooling, parents, and country. *Quarterly Journal of Economic Research* 66 (1): 180-186.

Gang, I.N., and K.F. Zimmerman. 2000. Is child like parent? Educational attainment and ethnic origin. *Journal of Human Resources* 35 (3): 550-69.

Gonzalez, A. 2003. The education and wages of immigrant children: The impact of age at arrival. *Economics of Education Review* 22 (2): 203-212.

Glick, J.E., and M.J. White. 2003a. The academic trajectories of immigrant youth: Analysis within and across cohorts. *Demography* 40(4): 759-783.

Glick, J.E., and M.J. White. 2003b. Post-secondary school participation of immigrant and native youth: The role of familial resources and educational expectations. *Social Science Research* (forthcoming).

Grant, L., and X.L. Rong. 1999. Gender, immigrant generation, ethnicity and the schooling progress of youth. *Journal of Research and Development in Education* 33 (1): 15-26.

Grenier, G. 1984. The effect of language characteristics on the wages of Hispanic American males. *Journal of Human Resources* 19 (1): 35-52.

Han, W., and J. Waldfogel. 2001. Child care costs and women's employment: A comparison of single and married mothers with preschool aged children. *Social Science Quarterly* 82(3): 552-68.

Hanushek, E.A. 1992. The trade-off between child quantity and quality. *Journal of Political Economy* 100 (1): 84-117.

Hart-Gonzalez, L., and S. Lindemann. 1993. Expected achievement in speaking proficiency, 1993. School of Language Studies, Foreign Services Institute, U.S. Department of State, *mimeo.*

Hashmi, A. 1987. Post-migration investment in education by immigrants in the United States. *Unpublished work. University of Illinois, Chicago.*

Haveman, R., and B.Wolfe. 1995. The determinants of children's attainments: A review of methods and findings. *Journal of Economic Literature* 33(4): 1829-78.

Haveman, R., B. Wolfe, and J. Spaulding. 1991. Childhood events and circumstances influencing high school completion. *Demography* 28 (1): 133-157.

Heckman, J. 1974. Effects of child care programs on women's work effort. *Journal of Political Economy* 82 (supplement): 136-63.

Hill, M., and J.G. Duncan. 1987. Parental family income and the socioeconomic attainment of children. *Social Science Research* 16 (1): 39-73.

Hirschman, C. 2001. The educational enrollment of immigrant youth: A test of the segmented-assimilation hypothesis. *Demography* 38 (3): 317-36.

Hirschman, C., and M.G. Wong. 1986. The extraordinary educational attainment of Asian Americans: A search for historical evidence and explanations. *Social Forces* 65 (1): 1-27.

Howes, C. 1983. Caregiver behavior in center and family day care. *Journal of Applied Development Psychology* 4: 99-107.

Jepsen, C., and L. Jepsen. 2001. Re-examining the effects of parental characteristics on educational attainment for a minor child. *Journal of Forensic Economics* 14 (2): 141-54.

Kao, G., and M. Tienda. 1995. Optimism and achievement: The educational performance of immigrant youth. *Social Science Quarterly* 76 (1): 1-19.

Kao, G., M. Tienda, and B. Schneider. 1996. Racial and ethnic variation in academic performance research. *Sociology of Education and Socialization* 11: 263-97.

Khan, A. 1997. Post-migration investment in education by immigrants in the United States. *Quarterly Review of Economics and Finance* 37 (Special Issue 1997): 285-313.

Kossoudji, S.A. 1988. English language ability and the labor market opportunities of Hispanic and East Asian immigrant men. *Journal of Labor Economics* 6 (2): 205-228.

Krein, S.F., and A. Beller. 1988. Educational attainment of children from single-parent families: Differences by exposure, gender, and race. *Demography* 25 (2): 221-234.

Lee, E.S., and X.L. Rong. 1988. The educational and economic achievement of Asian Americans. *Elementary School Journal* 88 (5): 545-560.

Lehrer, E.L. 1983. Determinants of child care mode choice: An economic perspective. *Social Science Research* 12: 69-80.

Lehrer, E.L. 1989. Preschoolers with working mothers: An analysis of the determinants of child care arrangements. *Journal of Population Economics* 1 (4): 251-68.

Leibowitz, A. 1972. Women's allocation of time to market and non-market activities: Differences by education. *Unpublished work. Columbia University.*

Leibowitz, A. 1974. Home investments in children. *Journal of Political Economy* 82 (2-II): S111-S131.

Leibowitz, A. 1977. Parental inputs and children's achievement. *Journal of Human Resources* 12 (2): 242-251.

Leibowitz, A., L.J. Waite, and C. Witsberger. 1988. Child care for preschoolers: Differences by child's age. *Demography* 25 (2): 205-20.

Manski, C., G. Sandefur, S. McLanahan, and D. Powers. 1992. Alternative estimates of the effect of family structure during adolescence on high school graduation. *Journal of the American Statistical Association* 87 (417): 25-38.

Miller, P.W., and Volker, P. 1989. Socioeconomic influences on educational attainment: Evidence and implications of the tertiary education finance debate. *Australian Journal of Statistics* 31 A: 47-70.

Ogbu, J.U. 1974. *The Next Generation: An Ethnography of Education in an Urban Neighborhood.* New York: Academic Press.

Ogbu, J.U. 1978. *Minority Education and Caste: The American System in Cross-cultural Perspective.* New York: Academic Press.

Ogbu, J.U. 1987. Variability in minority school performance: A problem in search of an explanation. *Anthropology and Education Quarterly* 18 (4): 313-334.

Ogbu, J.U. 1991. Immigrant and involuntary minorities in comparative perspective. In *Minority Status and Schooling: A Comparative Study of Immigrant and Involuntary Minorities,* edited by M.A. Gibson and J.U. Ogbu, 3-33. New York: Garland.

Ogbu, J.U., and M.E. Matute-Bianchi. 1986. Understanding sociocultural factors: Knowledge, identity, and school adjustment. In *Beyond Language: Social and Cultural Factors in Schooling Language Minority Students,* 73-142. Los Angeles: Office of Bilingual Bicultural Education.

Park, J.H. 1999. The earnings of immigrants in the United States. *The American Journal of Economics and Sociology* 58 (1): 43-56.

Perlmann, J. 1988. *Ethnic Differences.* Cambridge: Cambridge University Press.

Philips, D., and C. Howes. 1989. Indicators of quality in child care: Review of research. In *Quality in Child Care: What Does Research Tell Us?,* edited by D. Phillips, 1-20. Washington, D.C.: National Association for the Education of Young Children.

Portes, A., and R.G. Rumbaut. 1990. *Immigrant America.* Berkeley: University of California Press.

Powell, L. 2002. Joint labor supply and childcare decisions of married mothers. *Journal of Human Resources* 37(1): 106-28.

Ramakrishnan, K. 2004. Second-generation immigrants? The "2.5 generation" in the United States. *Social Science Quarterly* 85(2): 380-99.

Ribar, D. 1992. Child care and the labor supply of married women: Reduced form evidence. *Journal of Human Resources* 27 (1): 134-65.

Riphahn, R. 2003. Cohort effects in the educational attainment of second-generation immigrants in Germany: An analysis of census data. *Journal of Population Economics* 16 (4): 711-37.

Robins, P.K., and R.G. Spiegelman. 1978. An econometric model of the demand for child care. *Economic Inquiry* 16 (1): 83-94.

Rong, X.L., and L. Grant. 1992. Ethnicity, generation, and school attainment of Asians, Hispanics and non-Hispanic whites. *The Sociological Quarterly* 33 (4): 625-636.

Ruopp, R., J. Travers, F. Glantz, and C. Coelen. 1979. *Children at the center: Final report of the national day care study.* Cambridge, MA: Abt Associates.

Rumbaut, R.G. 1995. The new Californians: Comparative research findings on the educational progress of immigrant children. In *California's Immigrant Children: Theory, Research, and Implications for Educational Policy,* edited by R. Rumbaut and W.A. Cornelius. Center for U.S. Mexican Studies, University of California, San Diego.

Sanford, J., and M. Seeborg. 2003. The effects of ethnic capital and age of arrival on the standard of living of young immigrants. *Journal of Economics* 29(1): 27-48.

Schaafsma, J., and A. Sweetman. 2001. Immigrant earnings: Age at immigration matters. *Canadian Journal of Economics* 34(4): 625-636.

Schoggen, P.H., and M.F. Schoggen. 1968. Behavior units in observational research. Paper presented at the symposium on Methodological Issues in Observational Research, American Psychological Association.

Schultz, T.W. 1961. Investment in human capital. *American Economic Review* 51 (1): 1-17.

Schultz, T.P. 1984. The schooling and health of children of U.S immigrants and natives. *Research in Population Economics* 5: 251-288.

Stafford, F.P. 1987. Women's work, sibling competition, and children's school performance. *American Economic Review* 77 (5): 972-980.

Smith, J. 1990. *Hispanics and the American dream: An analysis of Hispanic male labor market wages, 1940-1980.* Santa Monica, CA: Rand Corporation.

Sweetman, A. 1998. Immigrant children in grade school: An international perspective. *Unpublished paper.*

Tainer, E.M. 1988. English language proficiency and the determinants of earnings among foreign-born men. *Journal of Human Resources* 23 (1): 108-122.

Tach, L., and G. Farkas. 2003. Ability grouping and educational stratification in the early school years. Department of Sociology, Pennsylvania State University, *Photocopy.*

Trueba, H. 1987. *Success or failure? Learning and the language minority student.* Cambridge, MA: Newbury House.

U.S. Bureau of the Census. 1993. 1990 Census of Population and Housing, Public Use Microdata Samples, United States, Technical Documentation, Government Printing Office, Washington, D.C.

U.S. Bureau of the Census. 1995. School Enrollment Supplemental Documentation. Washington, D.C. October.

Velez, W. 1989. High school attrition among Hispanic and non-Hispanic white youths. *Sociology of Education* 62 (2): 119-133.

Vernez, G., and A. Abrahamse. 1996. *How Immigrants Fare in U.S. Education.* Santa Monica, CA: Rand Center for Research on Immigration Policy.

White, M.J., and G. Kaufman. 1997. Language usage, social capital, and school completion among immigrants and native-born ethnic groups. *Social Science Quarterly* 78 (2): 385-398.

White, M.J, and J.E. Glick. 2000. Generational status, social capital and the routes out of high school. *Sociological Forum* 15(4): 671-691.

Zimmerman, D.J. 1992. Regression toward mediocrity in economic stature. *American Economic Review* 82 (3): 409-429.

INDEX

A

Acquisition, 3, 5, 8, 9, 10, 12, 13, 143
Age-at-immigration, 3, 7-8, 10, 13, 24-25, 28, 40, 43, 45, 47-48, 51-52, 55-57, 61, 63, 66-69, 71, 74, 77, 85, 103, 110, 129, 139-142
Age group, 2, 3, 26, 42-43, 67, 69, 77, 89, 99, 104, 110, 116-117, 124, 128-129,
Anthropologists, 5, 6
Asia, 6, 32, 49-50, 53-56, 59, 65, 66, 69, 73-74, 77, 83, 87, 89, 91, 93, 95, 108, 113, 117, 119, 121, 138, 141
Assimilation, 2, 8, 9, 10, 27, 139, 142-143

B

Becker, 2, 13, 14, 21, 23
Benchmark, 42, 44, 49-51, 56-57, 59, 65-67, 73-75, 83, 87, 89, 91, 110, 113, 117, 119, 121, 124
Binary, 38, 39
choice model, 38
Black, 19, 40, 41, 43, 47, 50, 57, 61, 66, 77, 80, 86, 98, 128, 129, 133, 140, 143

C

Census of Population and Housing, 31, 109
Child, 33, 37
quality, 2, 3, 5, 14, 16-17, 24
quantity, 2, 3, 14
spacing, 16
Child Care, 17-19, 86, 108

Children
of immigrants, 1, 2, 7-9, 27, 34, 79, 143
of natives, 8
Coefficient, 50, 56, 74, 86, 119
negative, 51, 57, 67, 74, 86, 116, 119
positive, 63, 66, 85, 89, 129
Cohort, 9, 47, 63, 71
Country-of-Origin, 3, 4, 11, 24, 26, 28, 43-44, 51, 53, 56, 66, 69, 74, 87, 89, 124, 139, 141-142, 144

D

Demand, 18, 22-26, 28
Demographic, 18, 31, 35, 41, 43, 47, 61, 63, 85, 103, 110, 116, 129
Destination, 3, 10-12, 21-22, 24-28, 141, 142
specific skills, 10, 22, 25, 27, 141
Dropout rates, 3, 6, 7, 119, 134, 137, 143
Duration of residence, 6, 7, 11, 27, 75

E

Earnings, 2, 10, 11, 15, 18, 21, 27, 35, 40, 109, 117
Economists, 3, 5, 7, 13, 21
Education, 1, 3, 8, 12-17, 24, 26, 32-33, 46- 47, 50-51, 63, 66-67, 74, 77, 80, 86, 89, 103-104, 107-108, 117, 123-124, 137, 139-143
parental, 15, 20, 23, 33, 37-39, 43, 89, 98, 104, 108, 134, 138, 140-141, 143
returns to, 8, 10, 17, 21, 22, 25, 27

Printed in the United States
32636LVS00001B/13-36